Fast Start
in
Real Estate

Fast Start *in* Real Estate

A Survival Guide for New Agents

Karl Breckenridge

Real Estate
Education Company
a division of Dearborn Financial Publishing, Inc.

Publisher: Kathleen A. Welton
Cover Design: The Publishing Services Group

© 1989 by Dearborn Financial Publishing, Inc.

Published by Real Estate Education Company
a division of Dearborn Financial Publishing, Inc.

Printed in the United States of America

     10 9 8 7 6

Library of Congress Cataloging-in-Publication Data

Breckenridge, Karl.
   Fast start in real estate / by Karl Breckenridge.
     p. cm.
   Includes index.
   ISBN 0-88462-778-0
   ISBN 0-79310-393-2 (pbk.)
   1. Real estate business. 2. Real estate agent. 3. House selling.   I. Title.
HD1375.B78 1989
333.33—dc19
                                                      88-39660
                                                             CIP

...to Maria and Jim Blakely
...to Marva Arthurs

Ron Breckenridge:
 Leisure Consultant

Brent Breckenridge:
 Lead Grammarian

Contents

Preface

Our traditional commencement speech to 17 semesters' worth of graduating community college real estate students always concluded with 17 variations of caveats, enjoinders and declarations, amounting to: "You have been taught only the state-mandated curriculum required to pass the Nevada licensing test. Good sense and the will to survive dictate that you continue to hone your knowledge of the real-life, practical aspects of our business."

One particularly inspired variant of this farewell sermon likened a real estate transaction to a Scott Joplin rag being performed on the full keyboard of a Steinway piano. The class by now had learned all the white keys; only day-to-day experience could teach them the sharps and flats of the business. A voice chimed from the back of the classroom: "Then why don't you write a book about the black keys?"

* * * *

This is the book about the "black keys." And like a couple of other books we've written about the real estate industry, it's light supplemental reading—written to correlate with the scholarly texts written about the "white keys." Some of the content originated in a procedure manual we wrote for a Coldwell Banker residential office that we managed in the mid-1980s. Our goal is to make some fundamentals available in narrative form, so that you will be ready to serve your early clients admirably and legally, and to refine your technique with each transaction as your feet become more firmly planted in the profession. If an element of the business seems absent from these pages, the missing element probably falls outside the "fast start" objective.

The Reader's Guide

Throughout the pages that follow, only four distinct entities take part in the mythical situations we're about to dissect.

The first is a salesperson, and the content is written with you, the reader, visualized as that person. You will be assisted from time to time by another salesperson acting as your agent (a subagent to the seller). The third entity is the seller of a home and the final is the buyer of the home.

To avoid endless repetition of the terms *salesperson, cooperating salesperson, seller* and *buyer,* we have sprinkled similar terms, with varying number and gender, throughout the text. *Seller* and *buyer* may appear singular here, plural there, and occasionally are termed *owner(s)* and *prospect(s),* respectively. The seller's home is *the home, the house, the premises, the structure* or *the listing.* Same place.

Salesperson is interchangeable with *agent.* Broker carries additional emphasis—the broker has a higher degree of licensure and is responsible for the salesperson's activities. We have used *cobroker* advisedly as an alternate to *cooperating salesperson.*

*   *   *   *

He or she soon grows cumbersome, and frequently only one pronoun or the other appears, with no particular gender preference intended.

We use the term REALTOR® to identify a person who is a member of the National Association of REALTORS®, and subscribes to a strict Code of Ethics. Please note that all state licensees are not necessarily nor automatically REALTORS®. Also note: The word REALTOR® is a licensed tradestyle of the National Association of REALTORS®, as is the term *Multiple Listing Service*®, and its acronym, *MLS*®.

A personal note: We support membership in the National Association of REALTORS® and are proud of our association and active involvement in our local Board of REALTORS®. The greatest boost a new licensee can gain in finding a foothold in our profession is through membership and participation in board functions and by using the educational programs offered by your local board.

We occasionally refer to the colloquial *your buyer.* The phrase invites a clarification: In many areas, that licensee who is showing homes to a prospective buyer is, in reality, employed by the listing broker as a subagent to the seller. The possessive sense of the phrase *your*

buyer is therefore arguable from the fiduciary and technical standpoint. The phrase remains in the workaday vernacular of our industry,
however, and we trust that with this explanation offered, the reader
will tolerate use of the phrase in an effort to smooth the flow of
thoughts from print to comprehension.

* * * *

Your homeselling clients may enjoy and benefit from some of the suggestions in this book. It is partially for this readership that technical
jargon has been held to a minimum. If you are so fortunate as to have
sellers who are willing to invest a few hours' reading in an effort to become participants, not spectators, in the marketing of their own home,
share the book with them. Some sellers may see themselves in situations within the book, thereby relieving you of quoting them chapter
and verse their functions during the successful listing, preparation
and showing of their home.

* * * *

We've arrived at a new threshold—let's put textbooks and state licensing exams aside for a few hours, and just read for recreation about the
business—maybe storing up a few pointers that will be of value down
the road. We welcome you as a coworker, and offer a sincere wish for
good luck!

1

Leisure Time

The noonday sun danced on the shaft of the seven-iron in the lone golfer's hands. The station wagon packed with nine-year-olds motored down the street near the fairway.

"Try not to stare, boys," implored the mom driving the wagon, her eyes downcast in pity. "The poor man's probably out of a job, and doesn't have the advantages your fathers have, or he'd be out working like they are."

A small boy in the back seat broke the dejected silence "I think that's Mr. Breckenridge, our neighbor. He's got kind of a job—he says he's a real estate broker."

*   *   *   *

No one ever achieved pleasure in the real estate business without spending more time—more quality time, productive time—at this profession than they expended in their previous line of work.

A simple statement, a little pretentious even, but words to live by, words to tape on your bathroom mirror and reread each morning. And note a significant word: *Pleasure* appears where some might expect to read *income*. The pleasure has to arrive first—the other can't help but follow.

*   *   *   *

Ask any sales agent, brand-new or a twenty-year pro, why he or she entered the business, and the answer is usually a resounding "freedom of time schedule" (not to be confused with "freedom to work less time"). The second-place reason is usually the desire to be one's own boss, within limitations. That reason, thought through, is basically a restatement of the first.

Style and motivation vary from one veteran to another, but most share one trait: a vow, usually proclaimed two or three times a year, to chuck the whole thing and abdicate to somewhere like McMurdo Sound to study the mating habits of penguins. Or something even more frivolous. This business does that to your mind. But the prospect of awaiting somebody else's five o'clock quitting whistle soon refocuses our priorities—a salesperson gives up time-freedom reluctantly.

The dichotomy is that for a group of people who prize our independence and freedom, we allow our leisure time to be slowly and insidiously usurped by our clients and our own inner drive, until productive effort is replaced by the mere turning of a crank, but with nothing coming out the other end. What follows now is not the advocacy of sloth we alluded to earlier, but a corollary statement to the Calvinistic statement in boldface type above, which also belongs on the bathroom mirror: *Humans work and think more productively if they infuse leisure time into their schedule.*

* * * *

The American work ethic is founded on a five-day week, relaxation after five o'clock and weekends off. That's the way most of us grew up— our dads, and later moms and dads, kept a schedule something like that. Dagwood Bumstead never clobbered the mail carrier at two in the afternoon in his frenzy to catch the bus to work—Mr. Dithers expected him there at eight sharp. (Obviously this generalization doesn't hold water in reality, but the recollection of a child ignores the segment of the work force that was on duty all of the time, behind the scenes).

During the early tenure of their new careers, salespeople have to almost force themselves to play while the rest of the world is at work (again, an oversimplification). The sensation that overtakes us when we walk into a weekday movie matinee for the first time since grade school implants the same guilt that we felt when we cut class for an afternoon.

But if a salesperson is destined to survive in our seven-day-a-week business, dealing with self-engendered guilt is obligatory. You will, early in your career, spend two straight weeks waking up every morning knowing that you have three obligations to fulfill that day, each of which will dictate the clothes you wear, when and where (and if) you will eat, which car to drive and whether you will be able to catch your son's Little League game at five o'clock.

This sort of a schedule, or lack of a schedule, if not abated periodically, will rend at the fabric of your effectiveness, your home life and your social acquaintances. Neither the human body nor the discretionary side of the mind can withstand constant pressure and obligation without respite. A comfortable balance between a pleasant but disciplined workstyle and the expectations of your sales manager usually leads to early success.

*   *   *   *

Putting the office worker's, and quite possibly your own former schedule under an emotional peak-and-valley microscope, we note a number of carrots are evident. Office workers are treated to five carrots a week, each appearing at, say, five o'clock. Past that hour, the harness comes off and their lives become their own. Friday brings a triple carrot—the end of the day plus two days off.

Our carrots appear more or less frequently, but definitely less predictably. If you glean nothing else from this chapter, train yourself to recognize the carrot, then take full advantage of it. It will pop before your eyes morning or afternoon or evening, weekend or weekday. It will promise an hour, a half-day, a day or only a few minutes. To maintain your effectiveness, grab the carrot and enjoy some leisure time, without guilt.

Develop a sense of the time realistically required to enjoy some favorite leisure activity—if you're accustomed to nine holes of golf a weekend afternoon, find a course where you can go off at six thirty and get in a round before your ten o'clock appointment. Take a long lunch and jog. If your car's dirty and you've free until eleven, stay home and wash it.

Successful agents have learned that we have to conduct our lives like this—we serve at the pleasure of the public, and we are amply rewarded for being available to that public. But we too have families, friends and ourselves, and who better is there to share our quality hours with?

*   *   *   *

Fulfilling the need for psychic centering by recognizing leisure time and grabbing for it is sometimes easier said than done, and a frequent obstacle was alluded to earlier in this chapter—guilt. That immobilizing aspect is easy to tune out in our own minds—for most of us it's as simple as thinking, "Hey, I worked all weekend; today, I'm mowing the lawn, while I can still get the mower through it!"

Valued friends (usually those in more regimented fields of employment) can lay a real trip on you, but only if you let them. While you're mowing the grass on Tuesday, your neighbor may drive home for lunch attired in his three-piece suit and look askance at your comfortable shorts and the glass of lemonade perched on the fence. Smile at him broadly, with the recollection that he was having a cold one on the beach Sunday while you were showing homes to a prospect. His assessment of you is secondary—you're doing what you choose to do and that's the way our business is. . . .

An annoying fact about our lifestyle can be a child's assessment of our work habits—they still subscribe to the Dagwood Bumstead stereotype. Our own children can be educated about our atypical workstyle, but many children of nonlicensees, like the youths in the station wagon prefacing this chapter, are surprised to see adults teeing up a golf ball during the "work week." More than once our own children were disconcerted because their playmates carried the news back to them that Mr. Breckenridge was once again spotted goofing off during the week. An open dialogue about our weird hours is important to their parent-esteem.

*   *   *   *

The message is important, and requires constant reinforcement: We work hard, by a bizarre schedule, to posture our lifestyle for a balance between leisure and productivity. These two motivators feed like carnivores off each other, and success will follow those who separate them effectively.

Communications

Fifteen years ago, a Roto-Rooter man labored over a sewer cleanout, pushing the boring tool ever further into the line in search of the tree root. Peering over his shoulder was a physician watching with great interest.

A loud beep emanated from one man's belt, and he excused himself to make a phone call. Upon his return, the other man asked where the beep had come from. The Roto-Rooter man showed the doctor the "beeper" on his belt loop, and at that moment an electronic industry that had been in its infancy came of age.

*   *   *   *

In some people's minds, the two crafts represented in the preceding slightly enhanced historical event are arguably the only two whose professional import and urgency dictate the use of a pocket beeper. OK, add a third—firefighters.

A paging device, in the current state of the art, beeps or vibrates silently and unnoticed by anyone but the wearer and utters a one-way voice message or displays an LCD phone number or message. On balance, and in sincerity, it can be a wonderful, timesaving tool for a real estate salesperson, when used with discretion. But, read on:

For those in the real estate business, a telephone call often triggers a sequence of acts that result in a commission, e.g., money. However, and probably more often, a page may be to inform the pagee to pick up a loaf of bread. We tell our spouses and the children not to use our high tech toys save for a dire emergency, but the definition of that term floats like the prime rate from one circumstance to the next. The husband who paid only minor notice to events in Chernobyl might set the pager in his wife's purse into a cacophony if he can't find his tennis racquet.

Let's play the scenario out. Across town, his bride is showing a home and the buyers' interest is increasing minute by minute. Hearken to—THE BEEP.

*   *   *   *

Both parties to the showing are at that moment compromised—the buyers' attention is interrupted, a mood is broken. Their salesperson's concentration goes from this appointment to the greener grass on the other side of the fence: She remembers the larger home she showed someone else that morning and knows that the page absolutely has to be those buyers, trying feverishly to have an offer written before their plane leaves town.

The ability to respond intelligently to the birds in hand is sacrificed to the other bush. No phone is available in the vacant homes she's showing, and her frustration becomes incapacitating. Her desperation finally drives her to go to the next-door neighbor's to borrow a phone to allay her anxiety.

In witness to what the page did to her effectiveness, analyze what took place in the buyers' minds: A pleasant, promising showing was interrupted. Most damaging to the transaction is the message she unwittingly conveyed to the buyers: "This phone call, at this moment, is more important than you are." Resentment rears its ugly head and unnecessary time will be needed to patch up the relationship. The spell is broken and a sad fact in our business is that buyers will gravitate away from a home they inherently like if they lose their allegiance with the salesperson. More unnervingly, they have been known to have another salesperson show them the same home and then make an offer.

For the sake of a racquet, a selling opportunity is jeopardized or lost. . . .

A final caveat for potential pager users: If you include your pager number on your business card, as many salespeople now do, you will live forever committed to being instantly available to your clients.

Prospects will call your office under normal circumstances and, in your absence, wait for a reasonable time for a return call. But if they know you have a pager, that reasonable time shrinks to the interval they think it should take you to find a pay phone and return the call. Whether the hour is between eight and five, or ten in the evening in the middle of a movie, if you are on page you better carry a pocket full of quarters for the phone. The commission that one phone call in a hundred may generate falls short of justifying the inconvenience that the other ninety-nine beeps wreak on your life.

*   *   *   *

The home telephone-answering machine deserves attention in a chapter about real estate communication—these devices, the bane of our clients a decade ago, are now de rigueur if used properly.

As we let our fingers do the walking through these white pages with a few random thoughts about answering devices (for brevity, we'll use the telephone companies' sobriquet *AD*, answering device), think not only of client-to-salesperson calls, but the more frequent messages to and from other salespeople.

First, let's dispel the myth that callers won't leave a message on an AD. That statement, true a few years ago, no longer applies if the AD owner adheres to a few self-imposed procedures:

Keep your machine in working order so that it answers after a few rings and transmits to the caller a crisp, lifelike reproduction of your voice. (Synthesized voices are OUT!) Tape condition is important, and the newer ADs accept replacement cartridges to easily replace the ones that wear out, usually after a couple of years. Get a machine that starts recording your client's message immediately after your voice ends.

Cutesy messages are also out—we've heard them all, from rap songs to Wagnerian background music to your day's schedule set in poetry—we're trying to sound like professionals, not Dr. Seuss. Out also are time-consuming apologies for having to use a machine or an unnaturally slow cadence to your voice, as if your usual callers are somewhat dim and you're trying to accommodate them.

Answer with a greeting that indicates you left the message recently, as in "Good Morning," prior to noon—or at least mention the day: "I'll be in and out all day Thursday." Your caller will know that you didn't make an all-purpose message and take off for Aspen. Then keep the message current as morning becomes afternoon or Thursday reaches Friday.

Tell callers when they may expect a response—you don't have to divulge when you'll return to your home, which many AD users resist for security reasons. We like "We'll check this machine once every hour all Friday afternoon." Now the fruition of owning a machine— the function that makes the machine work for you: CHECK the messages and RETURN any calls.

If your message is bright, current and promises a timely reply, first-time callers will leave a message. Those with whom you trade calls frequently will respect your track record and use your AD.

Upon initial contact with new clients where probability of a telephone exchange exists, tell them that you use an AD and pledge cooperation if they'll give it a try. If you hold up the bargain, your future business alliance should solidify, and you might just edge out a competitor who is habitually hard to contact.

*   *   *   *

Don't let all the checking in and changing messages intimidate you. It becomes second nature rapidly. Select an AD with modern features, available for less than two hundred dollars and simple to connect. The good ones allow for access from any Touch-Tone® phone, with different buttons on the phone keyed to listen to messages, repeat or erase them, or change your answering message by simply talking into the handset of a client's phone or a pay phone, locally or long-distance. When at home, we frequently use our set to record a conversation, not for sinister purposes, but to keep an involved message, numbers, directions or offer straight until we can transcribe it onto paper. It's perfectly legal—just tell the other party why you're making a tape.

An interesting feature of the newer machines counts the total calls to the home and also the number of messages left. Our experience, using some of the techniques above, is that very few people hang up when they hear our AD. The system, when used intelligently, can make a highly mobile salesperson quite accessible. Frankly, we'd rather hear a message in your voice and inflection and subtle nuance on our AD than the same message as interpreted by an answering-service operator reading the chicken-scratching of the operator on the last shift. . . .

*   *   *   *

The third option on our menu for staying in touch in style is the steak and lobster tail entree: the mobile phone, tucked in the trunk of a car with a handset on the dashboard or, more and more frequently, packed into a briefcase. Pagers and ADs are commonplace—mobile phones are less prevalent in the business, due to fairly high acquisition cost and per-message use charges. As the cellular system enters new market areas and as mobile-phone costs diminish, we'll probably find more and more of our associates "going mobile."

The necessity of a mobile unit rests somewhere in an equation factoring in daily commuting time and the radius of the market served, tempered by personal preference. For some of us, in certain markets, a mobile is a clear necessity. Others come to regard our cars as the last bastion of sanity and serenity and the only time we can think straight is while in transit from one crisis to another. The choice is yours.

If you opt for a mobile phone, refer back to the discussion on pagers, as similar drawbacks may apply to the use of a mobile set. If you're on a car phone, don't put the guests in the car on hold in deference to the client on the phone. And be ready to stop off for a loaf of bread!

3

Competition

We awoke in the middle of the night recently, snatched from the arms of Morpheus and a thought-provoking dream. During this nocturnal fantasy, a young couple in a ragtop Mustang sang "the heartbeat of America," an octet of Clydesdales towed a wagon laden with Miller Lite, while Ronald McDonald clowned around with a Double Whopper, pronouncing it to be Finger-Lickin' Good.

During the night the real estate agents had overtaken the Fortune 500, and were marketing the gross national product the same way they learned to sell homes.

*   *   *   *

Salespeople conduct their business in a competitive atmosphere best described as unique. We defy a reader to find another major sales industry in America that relies as heavily on the wares of another vendor for its inventory, or is as charitable with its competition, as ours is.

This chapter is an overview of our relationship with other agents— a sorting of the wheat from the chaff in terms of genuine competitive efforts that build business in a positive way versus efforts that tug at the will of novice agents, setting up all sorts of self-induced insecurity. Our intent is to posture you for success and to develop your understanding of valid marketing techniques as opposed to intra-agent intimidation.

In the practice of our profession we spend a large part of our day striving to increase our inventory (listings) and an equal amount of time communicating to our competitors the amenities of that inventory. A further observation is that no two of our products are ever alike. Almost every product in America for sale or resale falls within a model, year of manufacture, size, color or shape. But two identically built homes, side by side, will vary widely by the time they're a few years old.

Our relationship with a competitor, be it the agent or his or her office, cannot be likened to that between a Sony rep and the Panasonic man. Mr. Sony sells Sonys all day, and if consumers don't like the Sony VCR, they cross the street to Panasonic. Sony doesn't need a working knowledge of Panasonic, or vice versa. And a Panasonic model 5000 is identical to all the other 5000s in the warehouse, and will remain so five or ten years hence.

* * * *

Delete the proper nouns *Sony* and *Panasonic*, replace them with any two brand names in the Yellow Pages, and the statement retains validity. But plug in *salesperson* and *home*, and the rules change. If buyers aren't comfortable with our listings, they needn't cross the street to you. We'll show them your inventory. And there's no model 5000 house—no two are alike.

For this reason, we maintain a close relationship with our fellow salespeople. It would strain credibility to deny our intense competitive spirit. But to achieve success we're guided by the abject thought that the competitor we'd like to meet on some foggy dawn with drawn sabers for a duel to the end, might be the same competitor to get a call from a client an hour after dawn looking for a home exactly like your new listing. By that one phone call, your fiercest competitor is transformed into your closest ally.

By the by, to save you a worry, our disputes end with sabers at dawn only in extreme cases. Salespeople seldom get up that early.

So—our product is not solely ours to sell. Another means must be used to motivate consumers to contact us, and not brand X. In some arenas, a merchant simply pulls the rug out from under brand X with disparaging accounts of X's competence.

A compelling reason to avoid this tactic, aside from pure lack of class, is this: Assuming that you have joined the National Association of REALTORS® following earning your license, the REALTORS® Code of Ethics emphatically precludes members from denigrating the actions or competency of another member. Rightfully stringent censures are available to professional standards panels to mete out upon offenders. And many state regulatory commissions have adopted the Code of Ethics in gross, thereby placing licensees crosswise not only with their board but the body that grants their state licenses, and thus their livelihood.

Another reason to avoid this tactic lies in the possibility that the person whose character you impugn may later be the person who brings a good offer on your listing. Then you would get to tell the seller that even though you confided to them earlier that the offer's author is a dodo, they should now elect to let the dodo participate in the transaction. Fate is the hunter. . . .

It's a small world, and you're in a small town, no matter what size it may be. Play the game straight—win through skill and perseverance, or lose and move on, but leave your adversary's shortcomings, if any, to the system. The system works.

*   *   *   *

Two marketing advantages are thus unavailable: exclusivity of product, precluded by MLS® participation, and lowering the esteem of the competitor, regrettable in any industry.

A third method works like a charm—an agent can, legally, ethically and workably, make his or her name a household word. Many opt for a public sharing of their accomplishments, including everything but their 1040 in the media. In an effort to keep the novice from reeling in awe of the fellow agent's triumphs in comparison to the paucity of their own, we'll try to program you to react to the competitor's success rationally.

The obvious topic is the ''Million Dollar Clubs''—the denominator of the next few paragraphs. (Inflation has raised the ante to Two-Mil or Two-and-a-Half Mil in some areas.)

Respect is given to the achievement recipients when those awards are audited by a panel and the sales volume is verified by listing agreements and closing statement figures. The trend is to advertise unverified production volume in the newspapers like scores going up on a pinball machine in the corner deli. Regrettably, these unverified figures dilute the impact of the hard, honest, sale-volume awards audited and bestowed by an impartial panel.

The frequent, agent-purchased notices are sometimes subject to some interpretation. Did the sales actually close? Did the agents list, then sell their own listings, then take double credit? (Some do. . . .) How much did they close last month? Last year? We know an agent who listed a home, then sold it himself and later lost the sale. (Pay attention!) Then it sold again through a cobroker. The agent took credit for the listing, the blown sale and the final sale, and ran an ad extolling his monthly production as triple the sale price of the home.

The encouragement here to the novice is to worry about the big things, and such publicity is not a big one for you as you embark on your career. Every one of these dynamos started new, as you are, and the volume is out there for you, too. Go out and build it, like they did. Or *say* they did. . .

*   *   *   *

New agents are also intimidated by allusions to another agent's longevity in the business or the size of an office. One by one:

No substitute exists for longevity—all other factors being equal, seasoned salespeople are better representatives for their clients than novices, assuming they have been active and kept up with education along the way. Longevity is respected within these pages.

But some tenured veterans take the attitude that because their state licenses were struck by a Gutenberg press on papyrus, that fact alone entitles them to discount the talent of a novice salesperson.

The flip side of that coin is that many seasoned agents secure in their own self-assessments, will admit without much provocation that many, many people who have entered the business as recently as a year or two ago frequently have a clearer perspective of a certain situation than the veteran. Veterans try, deny as we may, to preserve the business as it was when we broke in. Example: We personally don't like open houses—we were trained to get the names of lookers and assess their ability to buy. Newer licensees, holding open houses with success, think a net should be thrown over us and we should be carted off for observation. Times change—we resist. You, as a new person, are well postured to enjoy the business as it is being practiced as you read this—some older fossils aren't. (No names, please.)

So respect longevity when respect is due for more than an ancient date on a license, and learn when experience can contribute knowledge. But don't be buffaloed—rather, be one of the novices we fossils frequently seek out for a second, fresh opinion.

*   *   *   *

The large versus small office rivalry looms large in all towns. Interesting here: The local agent's perception defines what's large or small. A major office in our town might only equal the farm club of a big firm's main office in a larger metropolitan market. A five-person office in your town might be the force majeure there.

Real estate ads everywhere extoll: "List with the biggest office" or "Stay with a small, personal firm." As promised above, the business will deal you a number of issues to fret over—another is not the number of people you work with. In our town we have large offices, some successful, others struggling. Ditto the one-to-fifteen-agent firms. We know agents doing extremely well in struggling offices and other agents having a tough go in large active offices. Have we now beat that point to death?

Affiliate yourself with compatible people, whether one or one hundred of them, working at a tempo you find comfortable. An office with training is a plus. Which suggests another perennial argument— better training in a large or small firm? It's a case basis—as a rule, we take our hats off to the large franchises for being the pros at developing aids and resources to get novices moving. The broker is the ultimate key—the human on the premises, not the policy set by a faraway Corporate Vice President of Agent Training. Talk to the human.

Our preference, you ask? We own a two-agent office, doing well, thank you, but we have not infrequently referred business to a local nationwide-franchised office when the nature of the client or the property indicates the referral. And they've sent a few back our way, for the same reason. Sharp offices of any size share the trait of a sharp new agent—success is out there to be enjoyed.

In sum, the only significant factor in the size of the office you affiliate with is the number of scores you can buy in the World Series pool. (If you've already chosen an office, we hope that you're comfortable. Office-hopping, even when done by a veteran, usually results in a two-month to four-month crimp in income and visibility.)

*   *   *   *

With some of the external elements of competition now in proportion, we turn to the only competitor in the business that can derail your productive hours. This little wraith resides within your own skull, goes to sleep with you every night and wakes you at dawn with a few worrisome thoughts just to get your heart started.

We keep our little guy off guard by trying to find out how many client contacts he made, in writing or personally, last week and by making a few more in the next week. We watch him start to slow down late in the day, and then we do one more deed that day than he does. Every time he cuts a corner, we stay in the lane to the finish tape. He forgets about an area of town or a price range when he hasn't had a client in that area for a while, but we keep our knowledge current.

The demon within slows down so gradually that he doesn't always recognize his growing ineffectiveness, and that's where we get him: We've learned to recognize our wheels spinning earlier. That ability is probably the only real motivational difference between novices and vets. All slide into bad habits and stagnation—vets recognize their own tailspins early, while novices mire themselves in deeper for a longer climb back up. With experience, the cycles come less frequently and we flatten out the peaks and valleys.

*   *   *   *

Many agents turn to tapes and books as self-motivating resources. The early tapes of a decade ago were dry, preachy and generally boring, and tainted public acceptance. The newer offerings are great and deserve a listen. Experienced agents wait for the newest Wayne Dyer audiocassette like our children queue up for Springsteen and Madonna.

Printwise, try the November 1984 edition of the National Association of REALTORS®' magazine *Real Estate Today*—it should be in your office library. It contains a 108-question self-assessment quiz by REALTOR® Ron Riggins of Macomb, Illinois. When our demon within has succeeded in fouling up our business productivity, home life and golf swing, we reread the checklist.

The questions are about the little things, so easy to backslide on, like returning phone calls, keeping listing progress records or daily prospecting calls and follow-ups. Invariably, in a six-month period we'll have become deficient in a majority of the 108 pitfalls and merely rereading them starts our inner pendulum swinging back toward center. The awesome visage of that movement usually sends our demon cowering for cover for a few more months.

Not surprisingly, the centering of our business endeavors brings life around the house and our golf game right back to an even keel...

* * * *

So if it's competition you fear, you know now whence the legitimate concerns start—right between your own ears. Forget the guys down the street—they've got their own inner demons. You just attend to the one reading this book along with you right now, perched up on your shoulder. Many of the aces up Lucy Fer's little sleeve lose effectiveness as you separate invalid barriers from opportunities.

A companion word to *competition* is *rejection*. The former occasionally breeds the latter, and our business by nature is the quintessence of a breeding pond. In this chapter some characteristics and sources of competition were addressed.

The process included two people—you and another agent. The following chapter introduces a third player—enter, stage right, a friend or relative.

4

Friends and Family

Hell knoweth no fury like that within your mother-in-law right after she backs out of the condo purchase and you tell her that there's no way she'll ever see her earnest money deposit again.

* * * *

To assure that neither disappointment nor rejection ever sully the positive attitude of a new salesperson, we advocate that you make believe that you, an orphan without relatives, have just arrived from the third ring of Saturn, knowing not a soul in your new world. You are not prejudged by the strangers you mingle with, nor do you have any expectations from them.

Expecting no kick-start to your career from any of these earthlings, your triumphs are all your own, of your own creation and never the by-product of an obligation or accommodation. These are the purest form of accomplishments.

The novices who can adopt this mind-set as they embark on a new career are destined for success.

* * * *

All that is a nifty idea, but we've yet to meet that cosmic immigrant. In truth, the basis for anticipating success by everyone who chooses a real estate career, including thee and me, is the broad range of friends and acquaintances we have developed by growing up in a community, by working among a large staff of employees or by otherwise being in contact with a wide spectrum of people.

It's a natural assumption that a percentage of those people will seek you out for their real estate needs and the law of large numbers guarantees a built-in clientele.

This book is founded on a positive attitude and postures you for success and within that context we'll agree that a fair number of friends will use your talents. But—consider some additional insight in homebuyers' and sellers' attitudes vis-a-vis the acquaintance who becomes a real estate licensee.

*   *   *   *

The name of the success game for the novice is an "up" mental attitude; a feeling of rejection after a friend selects another agent to help sell or purchase a home tugs that attitude down. We'll try here to offer a few reasons why things go the way they do, to defy that gravity. As a premise to start the discussion, we'll turn some tables on ourselves:

Most of us people-oriented types are friendly with at least five dentists, eight CPAs, eighteen attorneys, six barbers (or beauticians) and two plumbers.

Now the starting premise: How many of these people that you know, just as they know you, do you employ in the normal course of activities? The usual response is one per category.

We too are a category of professionals. You are but one of several agents that your friends know, enjoy as a person and have respect for. But the pathway from acquaintance to employment is circuitous.

Reason One

One reason a friend may employ another agent in your stead is a prior relationship with that agent. In choosing any professional, people tend to stick with a person who has been serving them well and their loyalty intensifies with the passage of time.

Examine your own relationships with any of the above categories of people and pose the question to yourself—if a friend attained a CPA or law degree, would your affinity for that friend be sufficient to sway you from your present accountant or attorney? If your accountant has consistently reduced your tax liability over a period of years, moving your books to the friend who was recently certified as an accountant would be a tremendously difficult choice.

Your friend who lists with a competitor may recognize the same depth of allegiance to that agent, due to a prior, pleasant transaction.

It's small consolation as you enter real estate that the same difficulty that impedes you in penetrating long-standing relationships early in your career becomes a plus later as you build a clientele. The clients you develop now and serve admirably will tend to stay with you for the long haul.

Reason Two

Another characteristic of our business is clear—the relative infrequency of a friend's opportunities to choose you as an agent. We visit a dentist twice a year (or should!), an attorney maybe annually, the CPA every April 13 and our barber every few weeks.

But pity the real estate salesperson—according to statistics, the average American changes her residence only once every five-and-a-half years. And friends, even very good ones, are unlikely to sell their homes just to throw a little business your way, as you might do for the buddy who opens an ice-cream parlor.

Our friends make many new acquaintances during a five-year span and clients who thought you walked on water when they bought their homes through you have probably each met a dozen other agents since moving into their new homes and towns. (The maintenance of client relationships falls outside the quick-start intent of this book promised in the preface, but is definite grist for a chapter in a sequel.)

Longstanding alliances and infrequency of need are two common reasons that we don't always get the business that we initially looked forward to. We'll now examine a third, then offer a few tips for turning disappointment into a positive opportunity.

Reason Three

The home of a friend appears for sale in the paper, advertised through another agent. Unbeknownst to you, your friend, an orthodontist, has put a daughter through Stanford by banding the teeth of the other agent's five children. Put yourself now in either person's place—the orthodontist recognizes an opportunity to reciprocate with an excellent patient and the other agent might not have been too bashful about requesting the listing. (We wouldn't be either. . . .)

The message in all three preceding instances: There are frequently behind-the-scenes reasons for business falling the way that it falls and like as not, the friend's intent is not a rejection of you, but a preference for another agent. The difference is admittedly hairline and semantical, but sufficient to remove the onus of rejection from your outlook.

*   *   *   *

Well, all this is revealing—we now have an insight into why another agent is dealing with a friend that we counted on as a potential client. But that knowledge doesn't further our goal to build business. What we need is a means of turning short-term setbacks like this into longer-term triumphs.

More often than not, friends will take the initiative to call you, and offer explanations for their actions. Believe it or don't, but look for this to happen. The friends, when they call, will be sheepish or apologetic, but cut them some slack—they care enough to make the effort, and it's not easy for them either.

Your friends' explanations for choosing another agent may track with one of the above three reasons or a variety of others, valid or abject. Your status as their future agent—or as only a vacancy in their Rolodex—hinges on your response.

A suggested attitude is a reiteration of some of the preceding facts—we're trying to make them feel good and let them off the hook. Tell them what we read here: "You can't do business with everybody at once"; "So-and-so bought her last three . . .(cars, bedroom sets, whatever) from you; of course you gave her the listing!"—say it and smile.

Then you set the hook for triumph. Assure them of your support for the other agent. Bring a client through the home. Visit it alone, if you don't have a client for it. Show interest. When their mood has turned from guilt back to humor, kid them and tell them they're off the hook if they send you a referral.

Several plusses are accomplished at once. First, you have eased your friends through a difficult situation and have taken the news like the lady or gentleman that you are. You have asked them for a referral, which you'll probably get soon—homesellers talk to other homesellers.

Most importantly, you have postured yourself to be their next representative, should they elect to relist with another office if the home doesn't sell during the initial listing period. (Ethics minilecture: We're not advocating interfering with the agency of the current agent, which would be a clear Code of Ethics violation.)

An unbelievable number of agents display hostility to owner-friends under these circumstances. The odds are overwhelmingly in favor of a positive opportunity—usually a referral, occasionally a listing. But always a continued friendship.

All in the Family

We proposed one night to our community college class that an exchange be created to supply expertise to families of salespeople who wanted to sell or buy property. We could sell your sister's home, you could help find my mother a condominium. (An ongoing challenge.)

The simple beauty of this whole program would allow our families to relocate, all the while leaving related licensees isolated from the process, and with some semblance of a commission possibly finding its way to our office.

After the program was implemented, in our fantasy, the Nevada Real Estate Division would forever outlaw dealing with any member of a licensee's own family within the tenth degree of consanguinity, which should include any relative born since the Civil War.

The lighter objection to family business is that the licensed family member is usually treated during the course of the transaction to frequent reminders of his or her derelict third-grade report card, his first automobile wreck, the turkey she vulcanized one Thanksgiving and just about every other transgression committed during their lifetime. The usual epilogue to this journey back in time ends with, "Why did I hire you in the first place?"

Aside from these pleasant reminiscences, another fact exists: You will be paid for your efforts. Or, you won't.

If you aren't, you have worked for free, which is sometimes preferable to the second alternative, being paid. Every other family member will learn that you dozed off for ten weeks and then were rewarded with mom's patio set as a commission, the very one they all had their eye on. Look forward to a cool breeze as the family convenes on Easter morn.

*   *   *   *

The above is somewhat true, mostly in fun and possibly overstated (or understated) from family to family. The next words are all true and serious:

The maxim "Blood is thicker than water" was coined by a licensee, hired and anticipating compensation from a nonrelative, but introducing a family member into the transaction. Intrafamily dynamics notwithstanding, our fiduciary relationship with other agents and sellers is severely tested by the desire to protect and enhance the interests of a relative. Most states require a disclosure to all parties that an agent is related, by any vague distance, to a homeseller when listing the relative's property. The admission must be carried through when the shoe's on the other foot—when writing an offer on behalf of a relative for the purchase of property.

Relationship by blood or marriage does not diminish fiduciary. (We'll explore that word in more depth in the next chapter.) If your contractual obligation is to a seller via your subagency through an MLS® office, that's where it stays. Your family members, choosing you as their agent, should be apprised of this obligation at the outset of the transaction and the blood versus water analogy should be defined in order to forestall future misunderstandings.

Many of us have used an informal, reciprocal agreement to conquer the problem of dealing with relatives. You list our sister's home, we'll show your parents a home. Somewhere, someday, financial equity might reign: if not, we've both notched up another sales experience and the intrinsic reward of some new friends.

Now, to a light ending: Ponder the feelings of an agent here in town who was helping to show his parents' home to another agent's buyers. The prospect, surveying the rogues' gallery of family photos on the mantel, rudely remarked at how unattractive the owners' family was. Some of the snapshots were of the agent's children. Another was of him. . . .

*   *   *.   *

The time is upon us—the initial thoughts within the pages thus far have been some intangibles of the business—that which is debatable, changeable, one person's impressions and recollections set into words, with the hope that some content will prove valuable. The text now sets a new course. In the pages to follow, we'll look at more concrete elements of the business: ethics and agency, listings and, later, offers—printed, contractual forms with definable intent. Supplementing the listing chapter is a discussion of what activity should follow the listing to produce the offer.

Picture in your mind's eye a home, preferably one with which you are quite familiar. Into this home place the owners—real people of your acquaintance. You are cast in the role of yourself, the agent about to list the home. We hope you enjoy the transaction.

5

Who's the Boss?

A big black dog loped in front of our small blue car recently—
instinctively, we stomped on the brake and threw a quick right arm
between the dashboard and number-two son.

The casual bystander might have been moved by the valor of the
aging real estate man struggling to preserve the noggin of a six-foot-
five college athlete, who was belted in anyway. Old reflexes die hard.

(We missed the dog. . . .)

* * * *

This chapter is about a new reflex, known as *fiduciary agency*. During
the next few pages, we'd like to leave you with a new set of nerve-
endings, synapses that will cause certain phrases, attitudes and events
to grate on you like a quartet of fingernails screeching across a black-
board.

We'll not spend the balance of the book dwelling on it, because
much has been written in books longer and larger than this one, and
trade magazines can upgrade our understanding on a monthly basis.
We will tell you that a fiduciary relationship was not dreamed up only
to haunt and vex real estate people—the doctrine has been around
since the merrie-days of Olde England.

This chapter is about fiduciaries and our relationship with them
in conjunction with other brokers, nonlicensees and ourselves. It's a
little about ethics and a little about subagency and buyer-broker

agency, with a hint of our business' recent history. If the words make you just a little wary then we've accomplished our goal!

*   *   *   *

A statement of concept is a good place to start. Our fiduciary relationship with a client charges us with the duty of protecting and enhancing her interests through the exercise of our skills. It also requires us to divulge and disclose to her all information that is relevant to the transaction. In our community college classes we embellished that last duty a bit: We don't prepackage and filter information as it becomes available. We disclose it totally and, through counseling, help her sort out what's relevant. What's mere minutiae to us could change the course of the transaction to her benefit.

Another fiduciary duty is paramount—confidentiality. What happens between you and the boss stays between the two of you. Decide early in your career to direct the frequent requests from nonfiduciaries to the owner/seller or other principal.

*   *   *   *

Note that in all the language so far, one word has not crept into the text—one that you were probably expecting. The missing word is *compensation*. Frankly, we'd love to put in black and white that the fiduciary is the one who is paying your bill—and about 95 percent of the time that would be accurate. But be advised that many court decisions and opinions have held that a licensee, when conducting his usual activities in a manner that parallels or creates the impression that a fiduciary agency exists between himself and a client, then becomes an implied fiduciary agent (even in the absence of compensation or the expectation of any). The message is, we can put our necks into a noose sometimes just by being a good guy and offering a little free help. At the earliest juncture of any transaction, assess where the path could ultimately lead and conduct your activities accordingly.

Another fact goes hand in hand with the above warning: If you hold a license, you hold a license for all of your activities. The law prevents you from acting as a licensed salesperson during one transaction and just a well-meaning friend during another. When you don the mantle of licensure, it stays on until you take a statutory step with your state agency to surrender your status.

*   *   *   *

Now we'll muddy the fiduciary waters a little further. In a few pages we'll look at subagency in more detail. When we get there, hearken back to this warning: Courts have frequently held that under many common circumstances, an agent who apparently owed a fiduciary responsibility to one party, in reality owed the same degree of allegiance to another party to the transaction. These cases arise most frequently in transactions wherein the listing agent locates a buyer for her own listing, completes the offer to purchase and secures an acceptance, unassisted by another licensee. Other instances (usually more technical) arise when a listing agent (the apparent agent) and the selling agent (the subagent) are licensed with the same brokerage firm.

We'll not commit journalistic hara-kiri by trying to address diverse and technical cases occurring in fifty different state jurisdictions, but we hope that by briefly mentioning the complexity of the fiduciary doctrine, you'll benefit by treading lightly when the slightest hint of conflicting responsibility is evident and by keeping your broker advised of your intentions.

*   *   *   *

The preceding thoughts addressed our relationships with those who are, or may be held out to be, principals to an agency relationship. Now we'll look at the Other Guy, the party to the transaction who is clearly not a fiduciary principal (if that degree of clarity can be determined).

We regret to inform you that there are a few charlatans both in and out of the real estate profession who loosely interpret a fiduciary agency as the right and ability to place both their thumbs on the Other Guy's throat and throttle him into submission to his principal's wishes.

That theory merits some comment.

In our research, we could find no state in the union that has not integrated into regulatory statutes a mandate that all parties to a transaction, fiduciary notwithstanding, shall be entitled to receive from a licensee the highest degree of fairness, equity, disclosure, integrity, diligence and probably one more similar word from each of the fifty states.

The fiduciary doctrine charges us all with obedience to the requests of the principal, and we saved one element of the definition to include here: We are liable to perform only the legal and ethical requests of our principals, those that are not in conflict with the mandate in the preceding paragraph. If the principal demands a concealment, misrepresentation or any other act that raises your eyebrows, fall back and talk it over. She may not recognize the import of her request and may amend it after you explain its implications. But if she stands firm, your broker should be consulted for guidance.

So observe the buyer or other nonfiduciary party now from a new perspective: He is not entitled to our skills, counsel and knowledge, but neither should he be injured by our use of that expertise.

*   *   *   *

Prior to and shortly after World War II, most real estate brokers sought contractual listings on properties to market and sell and for their efforts they negotiated compensation, usually a percentage of the selling price, from the seller.

Nothing strange so far.

The broker placed a sign on the property and ran an ad or two in the paper. Now things start getting a little strange: Another broker across town, who knew of a prospect looking for a home similar to the first broker's new listing, couldn't or didn't call the listing broker. An element of our current industry was lacking back then—broker cooperation.

We showed our listing, you showed yours. We were all probably working with the same prospects. They called you, then they called us, then they called every other agent in the Yellow Pages, seeking updates on new listings. We knew about your listings and you knew where ours were, but you never drove the buyers past ours on the way to show yours.

One morning a broker had an idea that forever changed the course of residential brokerage. "Why don't you show your prospect my listing?" said he. "If you sell it, I'll give you a part of my commission."

*   *   *   *

Subagency was born on that day. A seller hired a broker, and the broker invited another broker to participate in the transaction. The seller looked only to the original listing broker for counsel; the other brokers invited to participate in the transaction respected the listing broker as the agent of the seller. Upon conveyance, the listing broker was paid by the seller, and part of her compensation went to the selling broker.

More progressive brokers even began giving fact sheets about their listings to other, favored broker-friends (and withholding the facts from others less favored—the first known abuse of cobrokerage).

Apropos of nothing, we remind you that the world was still awaiting the Xerox machine and the Polaroid camera. A mighty man at a good Smith Corona could type about five copies on carbon paper. Getting the word out to twenty-five other agents became a prodigious effort indeed!

This practice ultimately led to the creation of the *multiple-listing service* (MLS)—uniform dissemination of listing information on a common form with favoritism toward none and on a real-time basis. The Smith Corona gave way to a PC, some areas unabashedly split a town into two geographic zones and soon someone will figure out how to bounce a new listing description off a satellite into a subscriber office, before others among us are clear on how to measure a split-level home. . . .

*   *   *   *

But statutory and case law have eroded the facility of the subagency system. We're finding ourselves asking each other tougher questions, most of which, oversimplified, amount to "Who's the Boss?" Early in your career you'll have to tell a close friend who is buying a home listed through another agent that, although you cherish your former college-roommate relationship, for the next few weeks your allegiance will be with a stranger—the seller. You'll feel then the emotional pinch that we've all endured for four decades.

A warning now: You'll hear soon the erroneous theory that the buyer really pays the commission. She places funds in escrow that are then made available to the seller to satisfy the commission agreement.

That drum has been beaten in every brokerage office and a good many courtrooms across the land and has been roundly and soundly rejected every time. Be clear on the issue—in the eyes of the law, the seller pays the commission in an agent-subagent transaction.

*   *   *   *

The overview in the past few pages about fiduciary and subagency brings us to a point where we're conversant enough to address another subject: notice. Notice is a legal word that implies the act of informing and communicating with all of the parties to a transaction and describes the delivery and method of that communication.

The process is changing—some brokers still hold the misconception that the flow of information must be the overt result of an act, e.g., a telephone call, Mailgram or physical delivery of a document.

We hate in this case to squelch a misconception, because most of us believe that's the way it ought to be. But we'll share with you the current, accurate legal opinion regarding the process, then conjure up a real-life scenario.

A good interpretation of notice is that notice to all parties is deemed to have occurred at the instant that one of the parties in the fiduciary chain has actual knowledge of an act.

Now in human terms: A buyer, having no fiduciary status in a transaction, signs a counteroffer in the presence of a selling agent (a subagent of the seller). This occurs, say, in Marin County, just north of the Golden Gate Bridge. Across the bay the listing agent (direct agent of the seller) is playing golf in the Presidio of San Francisco. Since this is a Saturday, the seller (the principal), who lives in the listing in Palo Alto, may be away from his home for the day.

Read the following words, be bothered by them and even take them to your attorney to confirm that they're correct, but conduct your real estate practice in accordance with them: The seller, listing broker and selling broker, each thirty miles from the other, are deemed in the eyes of the law to have received notice that the contract was executed at the instant that the buyer signed it in witness of the selling agent. Notice among fiduciaries and principal is contemporaneous.

OK—no harm done—the home sold, but half the parties won't know it until Sunday morning. If we're lucky, that's the case. But let's throw in a twist.

The Marin County buyer signed the contract unbeknownst to the listing agent. The listing agent's new friend in the golf foursome was moving to the Bay Area and wanted to live in Silicon Valley. Palo Alto would be fine.

If this book is ever made into a movie, at this moment you'll hear the drone of a menacing organ chord in the background. The listing agent shows her new friend the principal's home after the golf game and writes an offer. Maybe she's successful in locating the seller that evening and she secures an acceptance.

The home has been sold twice. Two agents, each with procuring cause in their favor, feel that they have found a ready, willing and able buyer and expect the selling commission. And two buyers each think with good reason that they have found a home.

A similar event did occur, but not in California, and after many years in the courts a state supreme court held that the first buyer, the one in Marin County in the example, was the true buyer of the property. Subsequent acts were done in good faith and without malice, but the overriding fact was that the subagent had knowledge of the fruition of a contract, and his knowledge was held to be notice to all parties.

*   *   *   *

The thrust of the information above is to entice you, as a fiduciary agent, to meet and exceed the expectations of the law as you conduct your business. Don't rely on a court opinion as license to delay or take a more convenient route when you are the possessor of information during a transaction.

In subsequent chapters we'll implore you to hasten transfer of information. You now know the law, but remember that you are entering an industry that has changed immensely. Others in the profession, the dinosaurs we mentioned in an earlier chapter, are not as clear on notice as you now are. The majority of the practitioners of real estate still await a signed document to appear on their desk or a message to arrive on their AD. Notice manifested by a vision appearing to them on the back nine remains a mystery to many of us.

Exceed the legally recognized requirements for the act of notice and keep all parties to the transaction informed every step of the way.

*   *   *   *

Winding down the chapter now is an important topic, one not easy to reduce for a beginner's book. In time, we'll all come to know the subject better—it's called *buyer-broker agency*, usually just called *buyer agency*.

At first look, the concept is hard to comprehend, because the entire concept is emerging slowly in residential brokerage. We'd be doing you a disservice to explore the agency in any great depth, but it would be an equal disservice to omit reference to it from these pages, as if it didn't exist. Buyer agency is out there, and it's coming.

Reduced to simplest terms, buyer agency occurs when a licensee secures from a prospect who is interested in purchasing a home a written contract of employment that promises compensation to the licensee when a suitable home is located and the purchase is completed.

The buyer pays the seller agent's fee or commission.

The seller continues to be represented by another licensee, who oversees her interests. She pays that agent's commission.

The phrase *the buyer pays the selling agent's fee* should leap off the page because it is the operative difference between a buyer-broker agency transaction and a subagency sale. Many of the inherent problems of subagency enumerated earlier are solved or at least redefined by this shift of fiduciary from the seller to the buyer, insofar as where the selling agent's allegiance lies. Similarly, the obligation for notice, diluted by court opinions, are reheightened as the agency-subagency chain is severed.

Now a real-life puzzle for you fiduciary buffs: You see a sign on a building: "For Sale by Owner, 555-1234, or Call Your Broker." Is "your broker" the broker who the interested buyer calls for information, who then calls the owner and agrees to help the owner sell the building to the prospect in exchange for compensation? Or is "your broker" the broker the prospect pays to arrange the purchase?

Your broker is a frequently misused term, as is *your buyer*—(we alluded to that in the preface). As licensees we should hear small alarms going off whenever possessive words like *my* and *your* precede terms denoting parties to the transaction.

Buyer agency, a widespread practice in the commercial and industrial brokerage arena for many years, is still in relative infancy in residential brokerage. Informed approximations indicate that five percent to eight percent of residential conveyances use that form of agency and most of those are pocketed in a small number of areas.

Due to the rarity of regional experience to draw from, we'll not leap into the fray by publishing what may be misinformation when transported from our market area to yours. The transition from subagency to buyer agency on a nationwide scale, predicted by industry leaders to be inevitable, should be interesting (read frustrating) to many agents. Our industry can be likened to a Navy Supercarrier—leadership and reality dictate a change of course, but a lot of area will be covered before the ship starts answering the helm.

Be content at this juncture to understand the foregoing account of buyer-broker agency, grossly oversimplified as this: a transaction wherein the buyer pays his own fiduciary and the seller pays hers—each licensee serves his client to the best of his ability, to the common benefit of the entire transaction.

We counsel you not to go forth and give such an agreement a try until you receive a great deal more information from veterans in your area. But do seize opportunities to increase your knowledge of the practice—you'll benefit in the long run.

A final chapter note, before we move on to the listing chapter: Due to the relative infrequency of buyer-broker agency transactions and the fact that most are initiated by veterans, the balance of this text will approach situations as elements of subagency transactions.

The Listing

The real estate listing forms the trunk of a tree, from which the limbs and leaves of a successful transaction are borne. That is neither the prose of Joyce Kilmer nor Luther Burbank, but the consensus of experienced real estate professionals and escrow officers across the land.

* * * *

The hard reality is that a flawed listing contract with your seller increases the hazard exponentially of winding up in a drought before the fruit of the tree, the conveyance, is harvested. On the up side, the listing is undoubtedly the only document in the transaction that you will prepare in relative peace and quiet, devoid of an adversarial relationship. Ensuing documents may be penned out on the hood of a car, transmitted in terse Western Unionese or done in the unique atmosphere created between the buyer and the seller when the former asks the latter for three loan points, a new roof and the remaining cord of firewood.

So write the listing well, and relish it. Change it, refine it and savor it, like Steinbeck in the Valley.

* * * *

An explanatory note belongs here: A major element of any listing is obviously the asking price of the home. The thrust of these pages is to explore a few danger zones and, within those parameters, to discuss asking price theory. This discussion, save for one caveat to follow later, is limited to the context of appraisal methods.

With that bit of housekeeping in order, let's take a blank listing form and track through the blanks and boxes describing the home. For sake of discussion, our blank form is the typical form used in most areas, directed toward the marketing of an occupied, single-family residence. Obviously, the format may vary from our area to yours, but most of the blanks, if not the exact sequence, should be recognizable.

Line one might be "Owner's Name." "Easiest part of the listing," we heard a reader say. Read on—what follows are not obscure examples culled from a century of brokerage. Overtures to these operettas have probably been heard in your own office within the last twelve months.

*   *   *   *

You are visiting a married couple's home on an initial listing appointment. Your perceptive eye notes a conspicuous absence of any garments appropriate for one of the two genders in any closet. The license plate frame on the Z-car in the garage proclaiming "Happiness Is Being Single" heightens your suspicion.

Properly, you place business over tact and gently inquire about the spouse situation, if any. If the response is anything but "I am a single (or unmarried) person," then both spouses, current residence notwithstanding, must execute the listing contract. You would be doing yourself and your office, cobroker and client a disservice not to secure both signatures. You would place yourself in peril of litigation as well.

Observe the logical progression: A cobroker shows and obtains an offer on your listing, which is accepted by the spouse in residence. Sooner or later the other spouse will have to sign escrow instructions and the deed, as well as a few other documents. If that signature is withheld, the conveyance stops, but the buyer has by now given notice on her apartment, and her cobroker, like most of us, has already mentally spent her commission. Go ahead, bite the bullet and spread the news. What will follow is not pretty.

A corollary to this topic might save you some time in the future: When listing a house and the divorced owner's decree is final, ask the seller for a copy of the decree and offer it to a title insurer to verify, while you still have the luxury of time, that the property settlement language is adequate to extinguish any interest possibly held by virtue of community property in states where that theory is recognized. Frequently an escrow is delayed by inadequate language on the settlement or a decree that isn't recorded properly. At the eleventh hour the former spouse may be approached to execute a quitclaim deed to straighten the thing out. The possible response is covered in our seminar, "Opportunistic De Facto Extortion."

*   *   *   *

A second variation of quasi-ownership is suggested if the Z in the garage also sports a bumper sticker endorsing "Divorce Never—Murder Maybe." The more prevalent overture to this flaw in ownership usually starts off with something like: "My [*mother/father*] passed away and I want to sell the home."

We know of no automatic inheritances and the real property of a deceased person usually goes by action of law to their estate immediately upon recordation of the death certificate. Relationship by consanguinity does not imply the right nor the ability to convey the deceased's real property. Therefore, your client at this juncture should have been appointed executor (distaff: executrix) if the loved one left a will or, sans will, administrator/administratrix, CTA—*cum testamenta annexis* (with papers accompanying). Only that person (caution: may be persons or corporate entity or both) may execute a valid listing. That listing may be ratified by the devisee if distribution occurs prior to acceptance of an offer. (The devisee, by the way, is the inheritor, but you knew that!)

Realistically, courtesy may be extended to the client and much groundwork laid for marketing prior to court confirmation of executor/administrator, but don't turn up the burners until the listing is executed. The old Anglo-Saxon maxim, "Where there's a will there's a relative," could trip you up at a last-minute hearing.

Note: Most states (check yours) allow offers on estate property to be overbid in open court. Your listing should admonish all agents that court confirmation is required. (In the same vein, offers accepted later should contain a conditional "accepted subject to court confirmation").

In short, "Owner's Name" confusion is not an isolated occurrence and accuracy is a building block for the information that follows. Many brokerage offices require evidence of vesting from their sales associates prior to publication of listings.

* * * *

Discussing the simpler blanks on our listing form would be tedious and space-consuming, so we'll concentrate on those that are commonly misunderstood. Forms vary, so we'll not follow any particular order. Note: if a preponderance of your sales staff disagrees with our interpretation, we herein yield in advance to your local custom.

Here we go, blankly:

Square Footage.   Simplest explanation: the heated area of the home. Garages, screened sun rooms, enclosed breezeways and many add-ons fail this test. Measure the exterior wall perimeter where possible, and add room sizes in upper floors where stretching a tape is difficult. A stairwell counts once only—the penetration between floors is a void area. Basements are arguable. If the improved area meets the "basement test" that follows soon, count it, then highlight the "Comments" area with "Basement area included in square footage."

Many brokers resist finite footage statements and add a disclaimer coupled with a mandate, "Buyer to verify," if the buyer is more interested in footage than the home "in-gross."

Gratis tip: Point out to a buyer that a well-laid-out, 1,800-square-foot house can have more utility and "flow" than a chopped-up home of 2,000 feet or more. Square footage is an illusory amenity....

Final tip: Sooner or later you'll see a notation "ft^2"—that's a veteran's shorthand for square footage.

Lot Size.   Footage measurements on a plane level with the curvature of the earth. A surveyed 100-foot measurement of a lot on steep terrain could require, say, 105 linear feet of fencing on that property line. We usually "square off" the radius of the curve on a corner lot and indicate its size as rectangular.

Most agents express dimensions of an irregular lot by starting with the frontage, or street, measurement, then footages in order from the left-front corner of the lot clockwise around the perimeter, back to the right frontage corner.

Age of Home.   The best bet is the lid of the toilet tank. American Standard, Kohler, Crane and Eljer have been accommodating us for years by stamping the month and year the fixture was cast on the underside of the tank lid. Assuming the lid matches the toilet and the bathroom wasn't an add-on, the home is probably six months or so younger than the toilet.

Building permits are occasionally stapled inside an unfinished garage, furnaces are sometimes tagged, or the oil-tank vent is stamped with tank gallonage and date of burial.

Bedrooms.   A room bigger than a king-size bed isn't enough. Look for a closeable door, a heat supply, closets with doors and minimum floor area and ceiling height for your area. You probably have a bedroom if these criteria are met. A window is nice. . . .

Bathrooms.   The industry is growing content with *full* and *half* designations. *Half* is a basin and toilet; *full* is stabilizing on basin and toilet plus a bathing facility, be it a tub or shower, separate or combined into one fixture. The dated ³/₄ designation meant a toilet, basin and only a shower, which in most locales has gone the way of the crescent moon cut in the door of our older listings. You will still hear it used occasionally.

A *guest bath* remains generically a *full* or *half* bath, but convenient to guest areas of the home. The not infrequent room-with-a-basin is called a *room-with-a-basin*. A bidet is an optional feature only and does not impact on the nomenclature. Usually it will be installed only in a full bath. A few years ago we might have said "always" just then, instead of "usually," until:

Our office listed a home with an add-on workshop, wherein the homeowner allowed himself a small closet, plumbed with—you guessed it—a janitor's (deep) sink and a urinal. We fudged it up a half-step to a "half-bath" for the publication, with some trepidation. Just when you think you've seen it all. . .etc.

Garage.   Should be 20 feet minimum depth by eight feet wide (per car) and encloseable by a door. Separate doors on double garages are a premium feature due to the added interior width. *Carport* criteria varies: usually covered, with at least two walls and a concrete or asphaltic floor. We see some god-awful structures passed off as carports.

Dining Area.   A true formal dining room has four walls and full-height doors (cafe doors sometimes), at least one wall capable of framing a breakfront or hutch, and overhead lighting. A dining *area* is usually visible from an adjoining room and hopefully has at least one nice unbroken wall and the overhead light of the formal counterpart. *Family dining area* implies informality, possibly hard-surface floors and usually adjoins a kitchen. *Dining counters* are 10 inches to 12 inches higher than standard kitchen counters and usually separate kitchen and family rooms.

Family Room.   The implication is informality, possibly hard-surface floors. The early postwar term was *rumpus room* or *game room,* and we still hear that occasionally, as well as a new, trendy *activity room.* We see occasional confusion here with a *den* or *TV room,* the latter being a pleasant euphemism for a smallish family room.

Carpet.   *Full* indicates all rooms, kitchen and bath generally exempted. *Part* lacks one or more rooms, probably with some hard-surface flooring. Specify that surface in the "Comments" area.

Flooring.   This is the structural floor, usually hardwood, plywood or concrete slab. Use *hardwood* cautiously and verify if possible. One hardwood room does not justify the designation. Warning: Architects have been known to lay carpet over ply in the center of a room, then ring the perimeter from the carpet out to the walls with hardwood—great, *if* the buyer doesn't want full carpet or hardwood when she remodels. Kitchen and baths are usually also exempted from full *hardwood* designation.

Tip: Lift, if you can, the floor furnace outlet to reveal the butted joints of hardwood or laminations of plywood and verify the type of flooring.

Window Covering.   Existence of some permanent window shading throughout justifies *full* designation. If your area uses *drapes,* fabric drapes with a few exceptions, usually in baths and kitchen, justify *full.* Levolors, louvered shutters and woven woods are premium sales amenities and should appear under "Comments."

Dual Glazing.   Requires the entirety of windows, not just the larger ones or sliding doors, to be glazed with dual panes of sealed glass, permanently installed. Removable winter inserts belong only in the "Comments" area and are non-negotiable if included in the listing!

Basement. As a rule of thumb, a basement is one level below the main (usually) entry level of the home, and below earth grade. Not infrequently a sloping homesite permits a *daylight basement*, with large windows and possibly a grade-level entry. Many forms are including this feature as an alternate choice to X under this category.

A *finished* basement should enjoy a stairwell with a handrail and reasonable rise-distance ratio (let's try that again: The stairs shouldn't be too steep!), permanent floor and wall treatment, overhead lighting and a finished ceiling at least 6½ feet high. (An exposed heat duct or sewer cleanout here and there is OK, preferably painted or trimmed.) Mechanical systems (furnace, pumps, water heaters) should be enclosed.

Water Heater. Caveat here: If your form offers *solar* or *geothermal* as a choice, confirm that the natural heat source is not just to preheat water entering an electric, gas-fired or oil-fired heater. Buyers become surly when three days of cloudy weather kick on the booster and spin the utility meter for their so-called solar heater.

The primary source of heat energy is the response that belongs in the blank. (Building codes in many cities require a fossil or electrical primary source for all water heaters, as well as all furnaces.)

Record also in your listing notes the tank gallonage, usually on a data plate on the top or near the base of the heater. Few listing forms include gallonage, but rest assured that down the road a buyer will want to know the tank capacity.

Note: However it works, it's a *water heater*, not a *hot water heater*.

Construction. *Masonry* or *frame*. Quite possibly your home is a combination of both; if it exceeds 50 percent masonry, most boards permit the more desirable designation. Watch the use of *full brick* when it's more probably *brick veneer*.

Roof Type. Straightforward as to *shake* or *composition;* be a little wary of *slate* and *tile*, as opposed to simulated PVC duplicates. Slate is slate, tile is terra cotta, and many modern roofs are simulated (albeit excellent, durable roofs). In a similar vein, simulations of heavy shakes are available (and are prevalent and sometimes mandated by building code in fire-prone areas).

Mansard is not a type, it's a style—the type is probably built-up tar and gravel.

Patio.   Usually concrete, stone or brick, in our neck of the woods. A wood structure is a *deck*.

Landscaping.   Watch the hairline difference between *natural* and *none*. *Natural landscaping* to most people implies some enhancement of native vegetation (if any).

Fencing.   A trouble spot. To some, a fence merely delineates the property line. To other buyers, it has to be a wall six feet high (the legal limit in most residential neighborhoods). A reasonable test is whether it will impede the migration of average-size children and pets to and from the premises. Suspended chains, split-rail fences and moats require some soul-searching.

Note the material and style: chain-link, wood, masonry (frequently in combination). Woven, picket, grapestake, slumpstone and decorative masonry are usual style variants.

Sprinklers.   Sufficient to irrigate all landscaped areas of the yard from permanent buried lines with valves, drains and a permanently connected water supply. A buried garden hose screwed onto a hose bibb at one end and attached to a portable sprinkler where the hose resurfaces falls short of most buyers' idea of a sprinkler system. *Automatic* implies an electric or water-pressure clock operating integral valves on a somewhat predictable cycle.

Air-conditioning.   May be *central* through the home's furnace ducts or, if the home is hot-water-perimeter-heated, then by separate air-conditioning ducts. *Unit* is a through-wall or through-window installation and, like the storm windows, becomes nonremovable if included in the listing. These units rely only on electricity. *Evaporative* units are good old swamp coolers, mounted through the attic, wall or window. Ditto on permanence if listed. (Don't sell them short—the good ones work quite well.)

Isolated alternatives in cooling systems include chilled-water systems, common in commercial buildings but rare in homes and finally the old water-cooled condenser units, illegal in many areas due to the voluminous quantity of water they first consume and then void off into public sewers or storm drains. If you encounter one of these dinosaurs, go for help from an air-conditioning firm to assess whether the thing is repairable in case of failure. Your buyer will love you. (Your seller may not . . .)

*   *   *   *

We've seen a few forms that include such nebulous and subjective data like RV access, cable TV, distance to buses, 12-month utility costs, horse zoning, insulation R-factor and the seller's golf handicap. These are treated as a group dealing with unnecessary chopping blocks, nooses and boomerangs, coming soon to a chapter near you.

Now, the fun begins . . .

The foregoing information aligns with your representation of the structure and mechanics of the home, the non-negotiables and rock-solid amenities. The balance of the chapter relates to the minor amenities of the home that foster more misunderstandings than the home as a whole will. As you read, note that the value of almost all the examples is probably less than one percent of the asking price of the listing.

Homesellers have an angelically innocent perception of what elements of their home they are entitled to box up and load when the movers arrive. During the tedium between the listing and closing, most sellers lay awake at night conjuring up ways of systematically dismantling their soon-to-be-former digs. Let's look now at a few of the disappearing amenities this insomnia breeds, then come up with a plan to avoid any grief in the aftermath.

*   *   *   *

The dining room chandelier is the classic "exclusion" to note in the listing. (Bear in mind, as we tour the home, the options are to remove or replace any excluded item.) What now follows is a gramatically derelict inventory of what is, in reality, real property, but frequently fans the flames of misunderstanding:

Fancy switch plates and outlet covers, any upgraded light fixtures. In the kitchen, undercounter microwaves, clock radios, blender units. Water-softener cannisters and piping fall in a gray ownership area.

Westminster door chimes, floor and wall safes, built-in speakers, brass door knockers (remove if engraved, but replace or fill the holes).

A myriad in the bathroom: upgraded towel bars, toilet seat and pulsating shower heads; ornate mirrors, wall-mounted scales and premium (e.g., Sherle Wagner) basin and tub valves and fill spouts. (At prices ranging up to $1,500 for a set, they invite removal and replacement with a standard-grade fixture.)

Within the bedroom areas, ask about closet organizer units, which have not been prevalent long enough to establish a precedent for fixed versus personal character. Note also any bedspreads coordinated with drapes or wallpaper. Buyers want the bedspreads, sellers want the drapes. Both desires cross the line of what either party is legally entitled to keep. The question of what stays or vanishes is bound to be asked by the buyer—seek a statement now in anticipation of the inevitable.

Moving right along, highlight woodstoves and airtight fireplace inserts, fireplace screens (if attached to the lintel), gas logs, anemometers (wind speed and direction gauges) and Chronotherm-type thermostats. In the garage, fluorescent lights and shelving and storage units. A special note about burglar alarms: Many systems are owned by the service company and leased to the homeowner. Confirm that these systems, while attached and wired inside the walls, are in fact part of the realty.

Outside the home, more gremlins lurk: upgraded porchlights and post lights, Malibu lights, mailboxes, permanently plumbed gas barbecues and custom-shaped but freestanding patio furniture. Statuary and the ever-present wagon wheels in the yard are always nightmares, because they start off clearly as personal property but with the growth of vegetation become so integral to the landscaping that their removal destroys an attractive element of the mature yard. In the same can of worms are elements like a screen door or lamppost with the seller's name or initial (and in Texas, we suppose, their brand, Pardner). We offer no solution for these hypotheticals, but do work it out with the sellers during the listing appointment.

Still glancing around the yard, cast your eye upward for a basketball backboard and weathervane. And to keep the list of things to fight over from growing boring and mundane, we have the latest entry for your negotiating pleasure: the parabolic satellite receiver dish. In limited West Coast transactions, they lean toward the personal-property category, so long as the anchors are dug up and the holes filled. Do reach an understanding with your sellers, however...

*   *   *   *

Our career-high, world-class candidates for disappearing real property are next enumerated, all from real-life and first-person experience: an air-conditioning coil and condenser, several garage-door operators, a heavy $600 wrought-iron security/screen door (known as a Door of Distinction in many areas, in this case a Door of Extinction), four pedestal-mounted (yes, bolted down) bar stools, a brass foot-rail (different bar), ceiling fans galore, a laminated chopping block set into ceramic tile and a janitor's sink. The coup de grace in this bizarre litany of larceny is a musical toilet paper dispenser that played "It's a Small World" as the roll was turned. The likelihood that two adults in North America could ever want one of these, let alone fight over one, bespeaks the imagination you must use to list the home, the whole home, and nothing but the home.

*   *   *   *

A unique category of property is labeled in textbooks by the English common law term *appurtenance*. This translates loosely here in the colonies as "something that packs easily, but really should stay with the home." Technically, although we promised in the preface that we'd avoid techspeak, an appurtenance is an item with mobility and portability, but has utility only in conjunction with real, fixed property. A few of these are scattered around your listing and should be pointed out to the sellers:

Remote units for electric garage-door operators do absolutely nothing, except when in the proximity of their own garage door. If the industry awarded a prize for the most accidentally removed real property, the perennial winner would be the "Genie." Pin down the valve keys that go to fireplace log lighters and sprinkler systems. Deep-fat fryers, griddles, woks and alternate tops for Jenn-Aire–type ranges should stay with the range. Ditto the Corningware pots and pans for the older-style Corning ranges, which could use only compatible cookware. The hose and attachments for central vacuums stay. Nutone countertop units (blenders, mixers, knife sharpeners, etc.) are appurtenant. Pool and spa cleaning equipment and covers must remain behind. Indeed, the set of keys for the home, garage and supplemental locks are more frequently misplaced during the ecstasy of moving than you might imagine.

There may be other appurtenances, if your listing enjoys some unique features. Advise your sellers so that they might lie awake productively.

One final note: Put yourself in the mind of the homebuyers, who have just driven three days to their new manse and may be presumed to be slightly irritable because everything they own right down to the coffee pot is packed in indistinguishable cartons. Give them a break—call it personal, call it real, call it appurtenant, but call it humane—leave them at least a roll of toilet paper by each fixture, and all the light bulbs.

*   *   *   *

The question now begs to be asked: Should the home be shown to prospective buyers with the excluded property in place, prefaced by a written list of what property, if any, will remain behind following the sellers' exodus, or should it all be removed from view, thereby detracting from the appeal, ergo offering price?

Arguments exist for both alternatives and the solution is usually a little of each. It's a case-basis answer, and the thrust of this chapter is not to offer the solution, but to get all the potential problems out on the table so that you and the seller can arrive at an understanding.

*   *   *   *

Prior to accepting a contractual listing, we ask the sellers if any persons have seen the home with the intention of purchasing it and if so, whether any representation has been made to sell them the home without licensee participation. (Translation: without commission.)

These answers often come to light after we sign the listing and put up a sign in the yard. They're usually prefaced by, "Oh, by the way...." As in, "Oh, by the way, we told our neighbor we'd sell their kids the home, and they've already seen it twice."

The kids have seen the home, not through your efforts, thus no procuring cause. Score one, sellers. You have an *exclusive-right-to-sell listing.* Score tied, broker. There are a variety of tiebreakers and neither party ever feels good when the match is over.

If the sellers warrant that no one has been given an early run at the home, the possibility that any person can make a viable claim to exclude the licensee is extinguished. If the kids have seen the home, and the offer has in fact been made (and the sellers choose to honor the offer past the time that the listing is signed), we enter an *exclusion clause* in the listing: "If Mr. and Mrs. Blank purchase subject premises, seller herein shall not be liable for payment of commission to Breckenridge Realty."

But we don't stop there. We give the sellers about a week to get Mr. and Mrs. Blank underway and write an offer. Sentiments vary as to whether we help Mr. Seller with the offer, but experience has proven that frequently he'll pay something, if not a full commission, for our efforts, and we'll keep him as a friend, make new friends with the Blanks and salvage a somewhat positive transaction.

A small alarm in the back of our minds tells us that our fiduciary with the sellers does not end at the instant that the Blanks make an offer, either, and we might be doing ourselves, if not the seller, a favor to make sure the thing goes smoothly. In the same vein, we agree in advance whether the listing contract will be considered fulfilled when the Blanks make their offer or whether our listing will continue in force while the Blanks' escrow goes forward.

Minor notes: The Blanks, at the end of the week, revert to being just another buyer. The existence of an exclusion must be displayed in any offer of subagency (an MLS system). And an exclusion may be granted to more than one party at the inception of the listing. (But for heaven's sake, don't use a different day for each one to expire—pick one day for sundown to fall on all this largess.) Minor note: It would take some strange and compelling circumstances to entice us to grant an exclusion to a real estate licensee. (Many brokers claim the right to a commission subsequent to the conveyance, if the purchaser resells or offers the premises for sale within a specified time period.)

Last note, not so minor: Bear in mind that soon after signing the listing you will be preparing fact sheets and fliers containing measurements, descriptions and representations about the home. Your seller will be privy to this information. Your liability is elevated if the seller uses your accounts and descriptions to induce the Blanks to buy. (This eventuality also follows through to *exclusive-agency* listings.) In these litigious times, we're becoming less and less inclined to do work for free that may later become cause for our involvement in an unpleasant dispute, and the milk of human kindness is flowing less freely in the direction of exclusions and agency listings.

The nicest part of the whole discussion of exclusion clauses is that they don't happen all that frequently and they can be a valuable tool to convince a seller, awaiting Mr. and Mrs. Blank's yea or nay, to get the marketing effort moving. Don't grant an exclusion based only on what you read here—talk to your manager for additional guidance and theory.

*   *   *   *

Early in the chapter, we alluded to a potential problem area arising out of the listing price venue. We have elected to leave the topic for the end of the chapter, because we don't regard the discussion to follow as a public segment of the marketing effort, but as privileged between agent and seller(s).

It is not inconceivable that a property owner will ask you to list for a price that your expertise and comparables indicate to be inordinately below market price. Some motivation exists in the seller's mind to obtain a quick sale, albeit sacrificing a good deal of uncaptured equity. The sophistication of the seller should be assessed and, if compelling rationale for a quick sale is not evident, apply the brakes.

Be mindful of the doctrines of duress and diminished capacity and if the subtlest hint of either seem probable, seek further counsel from a family member or other advisor. Should a responsible ally of the seller concur with an offering at the requested price, press on, but document the conversation and research with a statement signed by the seller and their ally that the listing is taken with the seller's full knowledge that in your opinion the listed price is less than probable market value. Ethics have been severely challenged by some of these awkward transactions and new listings beckon every day. Don't separate these days by sleepless nights.

*   *   *   *

As our listing chapter swells to the big finish, we'll impart two final thoughts, these appropriate for the *expiration date* blank on the form. The first thought is a reminder that most, if not all state regulatory agencies demand that a known expiration date be inserted in listings, at the time the form is executed by the sellers. Some say that listings that run to perpetuity, e.g., *"this contract shall remain in force until the subject premises are conveyed,"* are illegal. We think it more realistic to call them simply unenforceable in court. Certainly sellers should not be expected to sign a listing, then two years later sell their home themselves, and have the brittle, yellowing pages of an ancient listing waved in their faces with a request for commission. In our area, and we're told, in many other markets, a three-month listing on a residential property is the norm. Many facts on the listing may change in a three-month period, and extending the listing triggers the listing agent to update the information. As an example, the loan balance or terms could change during the original listing period. In our area, property taxes are promulgated on the first Monday in December, and school district boundaries (contained in our local listings) usually are redefined during the summer months. Wise brokers key in on such changes and update their listings accordingly.

Our second observation in the "expiration" discussion is a short teaser. We'll allude to this possibility, and leave it to your manager to give you the local thinking on the matter: The possibility is that the listing may expire after you have placed the home into escrow. At this juncture, a contract exists between the buyers and sellers, and if a conveyance results, you and your office will receive a commission. However, with no listing contract in force, the sellers are free to seek a "backup" buyer. Remember, they have become adept in the wiles of marketing by witnessing your technique, and at this stage of the game, a probable market price has been pretty well defined. And, one of Breckenridge's Laws is that as soon as your *SOLD* sign goes up on the property, at least four people will come out of the woodwork, claiming to wish that they had known the home was for sale, so that they could have made an offer on it. These latecomers into the marketing theater give veterans the willies, for all too frequently they make the request to the owners to get in touch with them directly if something goes wrong. And, in the marketplace of the late 1980s, things do go wrong.

Talk to your manager about extending the listing expiration dates on homes in escrow, at least to the nominal end of the escrow period. Most managers will probably agree it's not a bad practice.

*   *   *   *

The blank document we started several hours ago should now be nearing completion, and either a response or N/A (not applicable) should appear in every blank and box. When properly executed by the seller(s) and by you on behalf of your office, another home appears in the marketplace.

Now the real marketing effort begins. All of the knowledge and care you exhibited while completing the listing input sheet unfortunately goes into next week's book in the same size and format as the listings above and below, to the left and to the right, of the major opus you've just created.

In the pages to follow, we'll share some observations and techniques to make your listing stand out from the others. . . .

7

Preparation I:
The Structure and Yard

Unless your new listing is one of the few homes that at one time hosted tryouts for the vandalism team, it's probably within a few hundred dollars of looking nice to a buyer. Help yourself to a timely commission by pitching in, shoulder to shoulder with your client, and get it ready to show and sell!

* * * *

We'll look now into the successful agent's ability to transport the sellers' minds and eyes into those of an imagined buyer. The sellers will learn to look at their own home not from the perspective of occupants of some tenure, but from the perspective of the people who will soon be driving up in the driveway for the first time. Gratis tip: Unless the sellers watched their home grow out of a hole in the ground, you, as a salesperson, can hasten their mental journey from owner to prospect by asking them to reminisce back to the first time they laid eyes on this, their very own home.

Onward now—in this chapter, a fine-tuning of the physical structure, followed by two chapters devoted to those who inhabit it.

* * * *

Setting the stage: We assumed for discussion in the listing chapter that our home was occupied and furnished. We'll here carry on with that assumption and add another: The home is first seen by new-comers from the street. While a limited number of homes, and indeed most condominiums, are not impacted by "street appeal," the fullest thrust of the tips in the next few paragraphs are directed toward the vast majority of American streetside homes.

Let there be no doubt in anyone's heart that the sale is virtually made or lost at the instant that the buyer sees, for this first time, the structure nestled thirty feet behind your office's sign. Sure, the buyer may have heard about the home from a neighbor or seen it on the weekly TV "Home Preview." They might have found it in a supermar-ket flier or talked to the agent on-floor at the real estate office. They al-ready know that it has gold-plated door knobs, a self-cleaning kitchen, a producing oil well in the back yard and a one-inch pipeline to the Coors brewery, but the initial visual impression is the motivator that overrides all that precedes, and moves the showing into escrow, or back to square one.

So give the buyers a show. Ideally, and not infrequently, your list-ing will be in good shape anyway, from the street-appeal standpoint. But in the case of a small amount of indifference by the owner or at the tail end of a tough winter, a little tweaking up might be in order. The small things dull the edge of excitement in that buyers' car coming 'round the corner. Happily, those minor defects are usually curable with minimal, if any, hard outlay of money and, more often, by just el-bow grease.

*   *   *   *

Landscaping, season permitting, must be top-grade—grass mowed, walks trimmed, hedges shaped and trees and other vegetation pruned. The post-mounted mailbox should be elevated back to the perpendic-ular from the New Year's party; ditto the fenceposts. Window screens and screen doors should be in place and serviceable; window cover-ings, even though they're inside the home, should appear level or symmetrical as seen from the exterior. Porchlight glass should be in-tact. Check the roof and raingutter for irregular shakes, missing shin-gles and signs of leakage. Look for bent or damaged plumbing vents and flue caps.

Please—make sure the house number is visible. Remove the old, leaning TV antenna, abandoned when the owner installed cable TV. Get rid of kite strings and Frisbees that wind up in trees and rooftops.

Hide the garbage cans for the duration of the marketing period. Major barriers to first impressions are motor homes, travel trailers and boats on trailers—they visually "shrink" the size of the home. If the seller is serious about selling, a dialogue must ensue about removing his weekend escape hardware. We've found some stuff in a hardware store called "TSP" to be the greatest for removing oil stains from concrete driveways. The list goes on and on—these are the usual offenders, but don't stop here. Your new listing may have visual distractions unique to your area.

*   *   *   *

A case should be made pro or con regarding spending money to facilitate a sale, and this might be the place to raise it: A good rule of thumb is that a dollar spent in preparation for marketing should result in that dollar being recaptured in a higher selling price. A corollary rule might be that a few dollars spent on preparation that speeds up the sale are also dollars well spent. While the expenditure may not result in a higher sale price, an earlier sale should save at least one house payment, together with prorated taxes, insurance and other accruing costs of ownership.

Assuming that the interior of the home is in decent shape, and further assuming that your sellers are amenable to laying out a coin or two to bring an earlier sale, the two words *curb appeal* should be whispered in their ears—they should spend the money, within reason, on the outside where the home falls short. Paint it, prune it and queue up the prospects, three deep!

*   *   *   *

Having now insured an exterior sure to set the buyers' hearts atwitter as they alight from their auto, follow through on the inside and keep the adrenalin pumping.

A day or two after the listing appointment, when sufficient time has elapsed to allow the sellers to talk rationally about something beside sale $$$s, you appear on their doorstep ready to take a look at the inside through the buyers' eyes.

Success in marketing a home lies partially in your ability to educate the sellers to the fact that buyers tend to diminish the value of any home disproportionately for each tiny chink in the armor that they can point out to the owner and the salesperson. Thus, a missing two-bit plastic trim cover on a basin valve will elevate into a ten-dollar plumbing bill in their minds, and enough of these little annoyances result in thousands of dollars being subtracted from the eventual offer, or worse, a pass on the home entirely in favor of another in the same price range.

To do the best job for your seller, the necessity to attend to these minor glitches must be stressed as paramount for effective marketing. If the homeowners are handy with tools, turn them loose. Develop a knowledge of what makes a home tick and where to buy the parts and pieces. Be ready to help—give up a Saturday afternoon and pitch in. While most of our competition can fly through a cash-on-cash number-crunching exercise on income property, we've made a nice living by knowing how to change a Moen valve cartridge in a faucet, or some other repair job. Many successful agents have a trunk full of tools and aren't afraid to use them—when dealing with a recalcitrant or all-thumbs homeowner, that's sometimes the only way to get the listing in shape to be shown.

* * * *

Fine-tuning the interior is easy—just act like a buyer, then correct what's cost-effective that bothers you. Some elements for attention appear throughout the home: sticking doorknobs and hinges, missing or broken switch and plug plates, torn window screens and hardware, absent overhead light fixture globes and cracked or broken window panes.

Room by room: In the kitchen, missing range knobs and oven controls, cabinet pulls and leaking or broken sink fills and valves. Chipped tile or Formica (sometimes easily repairable); inoperative burners, fans, dishwasher, oven elements or garbage disposal. (Remember—most of our contracts now demand that the components of a home be in working order at close of escrow, so deal with the problem when you have the luxury of time.)

In the bathroom—plumbing, plumbing, plumbing. Basins—valves, fills, stops. Tubs—ditto, plus a working shower head. Check the caulking everywhere, "Dap" as necessary. Turn on the fan, if so equipped: It should hum or purr, not clank or stand mute. Sliding shower enclosures should.

*   *   *   *

Bedroom doors invite attention—sliding doors should pass cleanly and have guides in place at the floor. Bifold doors were invented by a man with a vengeance against society, and so far he's winning, wherever he is, and we hope he's where he belongs. They're not difficult to adjust, providing they're the better quality with parts intact. Check hinged doors for carpet clearance.

Glance at the wall condition in general and look up at the ceiling for evidence of roof leaks. A reasonable number of nail holes in an occupied home is acceptable. Fill in the larger ones, e.g., the ever-present void behind a door where someone pushed the doorknob through the wall. Blanks are available for these, integrated with a doorstop. Leave hangers in locations where the subsequent owners will probably hang their own pictures—centered over a bed or fireplace, for example. Ditto the ceiling hooks for plants.

Next, mechanical systems. Look for smoke residue around the water heater and furnace flues and burners. Check for oil drippings under the furnace burners, water stains near the water-heater relief valve. Start the furnace—let the fan come on and cycle off. (You may smell burning dust if it hasn't run for a while.) Try the air conditioner—remember, thermal interlocks on most modern compressors prevent the equipment from starting when outside temperatures dip below about 45°. Look for leaks around the clothes washing machine services—open the electrical panel and check for missing, damaged or crispy breakers or fuses. Buy a circuit-tester (three bucks) and check a few random outlets. Buyers frequently do this during a walk-through (in our area they bring along a hair dryer, for some reason). They're entitled to have all the outlets working.

Turn on the sprinklers, weather permitting, and note damaged heads and diaphragm valves that stay open when the electric valve is turned off (usually just dirt in the line that will clear if cycled on and off rapidly). Open and close the garage doors, swing the gates, ring the doorbell—whatever goes with the home, check. The effort is integral to the job, and you're saving yourself a delay at the last minute.

Some states are adopting a mandatory seller disclosure of defects known to them. Mandatory or optional, the forms have been available for years from one publisher, make an excellent check-off list and afford future protection to you, your office and the seller.

*   *   *   *

Unless your listing is of the fixer-upper genre, the above effort will likely reveal flaws that in total are usually repairable for an extremely reasonable cash outlay and the aforementioned elbow grease. The combination of money and grease produces a listing effectively absent of chinks on which a buyer can gain a foothold.

*   *   *   *

Alas, some homes do need repainting, some homeowners are willing to paint—and paint, in the larger scheme of things, is dirt cheap. Interior paint for homes for sale comes in three colors: Winter White, Antique White and Navajo White. And yes, each color is available in latex and enamel. Do encourage flat for the walls and gloss for doorjambs and trim. And don't paint the lightswitches and doorknobs, if you please.

Now—reread the listing chapter caveats about removal of excluded real property and amenities and assist the owners in the removal of whatever they want to keep, replacing with alternates where that agreement was reached when the listing was signed.

*   *   *   *

The labor expended will not take place all in one hour or one day, unless the listing is a real creampuff. Quite probably the home will receive a showing or two while the touching-up is in progress. How nice it is to represent to a prospective buyer that the owner has agreed to make obvious repairs that, if ignored, might be an impediment to the sale!

In most of these chapters, we have tried to throw in one bon mot that saves you at least the price of this book, and here it comes: Some listings will have one major detriment. It may involve a repair. More often it will manifest itself as an element of decor that is, to be charitable, unique. Or uncharitably, stone ugly.

DON'T ignore the problem. Secure from a contractor, designer or other vendor a written bid for curing whatever is undesirable. Keep the bid on the premises.

A typical buyer, unless conversant in construction techniques, will peg the cost of replacing the International Orange basin in the master bathroom at close to $2000. In reality, the job might cost closer to $300. The numbers and examples might be overstated, but we're trying to emphasize a point: Don't allow a sale to be lost due to an invalid, amateur estimate. Prepare in advance an accurate cost for conquering inevitable resistance.

*   *   *   *

The physical element of the new listing is emerging like the monarch from its cocoon—the bug you visited on the initial listing appointment now stands pictured in the latest book as a butterfly. The exterior presence is first-rate and St. Elmo's fire fairly haloes around the steel frame of your For Sale sign. In the following two chapters, we'll attend to the owners' personal property within the listing.

"A little tweaking up may be in order...."

8

Preparation II:
The Excess and Offensive

If your sales affiliates tour your new listing and return to your office with a vivid recollection of the sixty-two bowling trophies in the den, but no memory of the premium ceramic tile in the entry, then you, as the listing agent, should place a paperclip on this page and immediately hand the book to the homeowners.

*   *   *   *

By and large, homes for sale are static and immobile, undaunted and unemotional about their destiny. Would that the owner of the home were so docile.

A couple selling their home invariably seizes the opportunity to showcase their many and diverse accomplishments and their personal causes and beliefs for the edification of the strangers who will soon be traversing their home. The guy who played college baseball will transform the family room into a miniature Cooperstown Hall of Fame, displaying trophies, caps, autographed balls, bronzed mitts and himself, posing with Willie Mays at the Rotary banquet. His bride, adept at crewelwork, might emblazon an entire wall with a ping-pong-table-sized panorama of Nantucket Harbor lobster boats lying at their moorings.

Wrong.

We invite your attention back to the opening line of this chapter and suggest that you offer the book to the homeowners—as they read what follows, they'll know why you loaned it to them and they'll take offense with us, not you.

The fact is, we're selling the house, and upon close of escrow, Nantucket Harbor and ol' number 24 will go with the owners. What's left is the house. Let's show the buyers the house itself with as little distraction as possible.

The owners' personality is a large part of the amenity of the home and tasteful decor and furnishings will always triumph over a hodge-podge of clutter. Nice furnishings sell houses—if that weren't true, the new tract model homes wouldn't be decorated so lavishly.

*   *   *   *

But a distinction must be drawn between attractive decor and expressions of the owners' personal taste. That threshold is subtle, and examples become vague in description, but usually fall within two categories:

First, the extreme expression of the owners' likes and hobbies, to the degree that the expression dominates the visiting buyers' attention. Real-life example: A seller friend of ours was totally engrossed in model trains as a hobby. Throughout his home were operating layouts, trackside photos and various mementos from the ribbons of steel. (Notably absent was our own favorite railroad slogan, ''Lead him into the roundhouse, Nellie, he'll never corner you there!'')

The home was as nice as any we've ever listed. But after one showing, the prospects left the home and their prevailing recollection was the obsession with railroading—premium features within the home were totally overlooked.

We got the momentum back on track (pun intended) on the second showing and sold the home, but the overwhelming decor had a detrimental effect on the progress of the sale. The message here: Undecorating the home during marketing, as onerous as that might be for the owners, occasionally benefits them. It is your sad task to suggest alterations where they are in the best interests of the sale.

A second category of decor and expression is a little tougher to deal with: a display in the home of subject matter that may offend some segment of the homebuying public.

Prospective buyers sometimes react irrationally to some homeowner's personal beliefs as displayed in the home. Some buyers, from time to time, might even refuse to deal with the owner.

Our personal feelings are not involved, confirmed, denied or even relevant to the following comments, but we offer these observations from real-life experiences, for what they are worth:

The most prevalent examples may be found in the lair of many red-blooded American teenage males. Misses June, October and May tacked to every plane surface in their bedrooms, surrounded by posters of rock music stars clad in strange, metallic garments and bumper stickers combining Anglo-Saxon words into clever but unpublishable maxims. The youthful buyer-parents vow: "We'll never permit that when OUR child reaches that age." Right on....

Other incidences, in no particular order and absent of personal agreement but guaranteed to be touchy, include: a large display of mounted game animal heads, quintessential proof that the seller is a wanton slayer; widespread documentation of trade-union activity; right-to-life pamphlets; and extensive ethnic, religious or national-origin memorabilia (we said extensive). Political preferences can be volatile—a candidate's campaign sign in the listing's front yard is taboo during the marketing period; moreover, it distracts from your For Sale sign.

Further demonstration of how deeply feelings can run, and the strange things that can invite unforeseen anxiety: A prospect, some time ago, took offense at our seller's fur coats hanging in the closet and immediately left our listing (a home she otherwise loved). We support species conservation personally, but abandoning a desirable home seemed a foolish way to demonstrate her displeasure.

We related this anecdote in class one evening and learned that years ago a Volkswagen parked in a seller's garage could instill the same negative emotion. How times change!

*   *   *   *

In the final evaluation the ideal home to show would be beautifully decorated, albeit with eminently forgettable appointments, so that the essence of the home prevails. And it would be occupied by sellers whose taste ran to the absolute middle of the road, right down to every picture on the wall, cartoon on the refrigerator door and magazine on the coffee table.

A reasonable approach to that nirvana will result in marketing success for you and your client.

*   *   *   *

The homesellers may inquire as to how they might occupy themselves during the showing appointment. Their function is easily stated: leave. We suggest sugar coating that response just a touch—perhaps the next paragraphs will help you explain to the owners why you'd like the home to yourself.

Unless the prospects are just plain rude, invariably they will hesitate to verbalize their objections about the home (if any) if the owners are present. By common courtesy, habit and in truth, they are guests in the home and are justifiably reluctant to make disparaging remarks around their "hosts."

If the owners have absented themselves by taking a walk, a ride or they just happen to be out anyway, the prospects might be more inclined to put into words an objection to a feature within the home. Then you, with a facility that grows with experience, will have the opportunity to overcome any negative impression.

That act is the essence of real estate sales. The positive points within a listing are obvious—it is the act of overcoming the negatives in an ethical fashion that separates the true salesperson from just an agent who has picked up a key.

Hearken back to the suggestion that bids are secured and available for the hard cost of curing anticipated resistance. With skill an agent may offer an option or revision that is economically feasible and thus mitigate the objection.

Now—if the owners are home, waiting in an adjoining room, your prospects' criticism and your suggestion for a fix may never surface or get resolved.

*   *   *   *

A final comment, this on a serious note regarding an admonishment we still hear all too frequently in this enlightened age: "We'd rather our home not be shown to. . . ." Fill in the blank: race, color, religion, creed, origin, couple with children, Raider fan—take your pick. The usual justification is that it's a courtesy to elderly neighbors who don't abide small children, or a myriad of other reasons that generally make no sense. All unlatch the door to the licensee's worst nightmare—federal and/or state discrimination charges, potentially resulting in your premature exit from the business.

This request cannot be honored, and rightfully so. A brief dialogue with the owners, apprising them of the import of their request and the legal peril they place themselves in, will usually bring them right around. Should they hold firm in their conviction, the words appearing in the listing chapter echo: A new listing beckons every day—don't separate those days by sleepless nights. Bail out....

*   *   *   *

Personal note: The preceding words were included in our rough manuscript, then almost omitted from the final version, due to the infrequency of the request. We concluded that those attitudes were but a distant memory from our early career.

Unfortunately, a week before the chapter was final, we heard them once again.

*   *   *   *

Our homeowner has gradually become a homeseller, two distinct types of folks. Frequently at this stage of a transaction these two personalities, sharing one body, are also spending their idle time looking at new homes to replace the one you are about to sell. This third personality, the buyer, lurking within the cranium of the owner-seller, raises good-natured suburban schizophrenia to an art form.

It is while working with these bifurcated individuals on both a sale and purchase simultaneously that novice salespeople receive their baptism by fire. A crack in the wall of a seller's home is minor, nitpicking—and its mere mention constitutes an insult to him. The identical crack in a home he is scrutinizing to purchase, however, ranks in his mind as a gulf big enough to challenge Evel Knievel.

A subtle attitude adjustment is required when your homeselling client wants to look at a few homes. As a seller, she has designated you and your office as her agent and your fiduciary runs to her. When you both step into the home that she may be interested in buying (in the absence of a buyer-broker agency with her), your allegiance transfers to the listing agent and the seller of that home. Your own seller-client should be informed in cordial but certain terms of the two hats you wear during the two separate transactions—her sale and her purchase.

Terminating this brief foray into the mind of the seller/buyer/owner-composite humanoid, we'll move to a companion chapter, still discussing personal property, but property of a less intense, less inflammatory nature—the property normal to any home for sale.

"And this is the master bedroom. . . ."

9

Preparation III: Typical Furnishings

In the year 2005 the last steel refrigerator was built—from that year forth the appliances were built from a derivative of the thermoplastic that earlier replaced the metal skin on airliners. By 2012 western civilization was brought to its knees: Pictures of ancestors were lost, intrafamily communication suspended, overnutrition warnings unavailable and grocery stores closed for lack of consumers' shopping lists.

What the bomb couldn't accomplish, the synthetic refrigerators did: Magnets wouldn't stick to their doors.

* * * *

A subtle shift in emphasis now, from excess and offensive personal property in your listing, to the normal furniture in a normal home—possessions that will be visible during a showing appointment and will enhance or detract from the ambiance of the home.

We borrow a page from the tract developer's book. Developers are very, very good at merchandising homes, and we learn from them. (Their obvious advantage is a supremely controllable selling environment—no one sleeps, cooks or bathes in their model homes.) Unfortunately, our only listings wherein no one sleeps, slurps or showers are typically also vacant of furniture—a condition that departs from the scenario this book is structured upon.

The page we borrow is the one that suggests a reasonable inclusion of personal property, be it magazines, ashtrays, plants, firewood, soap in the bathroom soap dish, a hat on the hall tree and on, on, on. Putting it bluntly, a model home appointed with nothing but what's on the floor at a furniture store, albeit top-of-the-line merchandise, would look, well, ethereal. If you doubt that, study most furniture-store displays—some intangible character is missing: the human element.

The tract developers know how to take the extra step of visualizing the knickknacks lying about an actual home and artistically clutter up the model just a bit.

Glance around your listing, using the tract model as a barometer of the direction you should take for pre-showing preparation. The chances are good that the homeowner gravitates toward the center of the decorating spectrum—orderly yet humanized. If so, count your blessings, offer a compliment and go directly to the next chapter.

*   *   *   *

Many homeowners, anticipating showing their home to prospects, make an attempt to sterilize it, to the detriment of your efforts. In some listings we have had to ask the owners to allow the museum frigidity to warm to the typical US of A family home atmosphere, however that quality might be defined. Strangely enough, suggesting a controlled trashing is as hard as its corollary request (when the listing is anything but sterile): an ever-so-slight hint in favor of a bit of housekeeping. Like maybe rolling the Harley out of the spare bedroom for a time, or taking the gerbils outside to enjoy the spring sun. Favorite personal example: In a friend's otherwise superior rural listing, a blue-light patio Bug-Zapper was suspended 'tween the kitchen and the dinette, primed to snap away at uninvited little diners. We suggested that better window screens might be a more marketable, albeit less dramatic, way to ward off our high-desert critters.

Bad housekeeping is not hard to recognize and requires little discussion here—messy houses don't sell readily, nor do cluttered ones. Owner cooperation is vital and must be secured.

So encourage the family to enjoy their home during the marketing period—a little straightening is nice, but most buyers recognize that beds don't always get made, and some dishes stay in the sink occasionally. Little boys tack Top Gun airplane posters on the wall, little girls counter with Top Gun pilots and parents don't always put their toys away either. That's called a *family home*, and potential buyers probably live the same way themselves.

*   *   *   *

Departing from nonfurniture bric-a-brac now being adjusted to an acceptable level through your subtle guile, turn your attention to the furniture proper. We personally would prefer to show a furnished home than one that's new or vacant, unless the owners' furniture is inordinately out of place in the home. Yet even within a tastefully furnished home, less is usually more.

Our experience is that homeowners tend to accumulate furniture, placing it in addition to rather than in lieu of existing furnishings. Strange are the ways we all come by our furnishings—frequently an item is offered by a friend, or we're storing it for someone who never retrieves it or we dig an extra chair out of the basement for a bridge party and don't quite get around to hauling it back downstairs.

Often a piece in a room is extraneous to the function of the room—an Exercycle® in a bedroom, a couple of TV trays kept available in the family room or a card table set up to do the taxes on. After a time, these interlopers begin acquiring an element of permanence. The card table accumulates magazines and a lamp and the TV trays soon host a plant or two. Our personal experience is that an exercise machine brings much more gratification when used as a coat rack rather than an aerobic appliance.

The point is that your listing probably includes at least one item of furniture per room that could be removed prior to showing the home, with little inconvenience to the seller. Every stray that the seller can temporarily live without will benefit the marketing by "opening up" the room and optically creating a more expansive home.

*   *   *   *

If the sellers want to participate in a little legerdemain with tasteful decorating, a productive venue might well be in the kitchen. Kitchens are fun, hopefully bright rooms—a wide variety of appointments are available to enhance kitchens and adjoining dining areas.

Buyers zero in on kitchens because a good part of their waking hours are spent in the kitchen/dinette area and the traffic flow and storage are important to them. The kitchen, like the bathroom, is one of the few rooms in the home that is prearranged. Other rooms transform with the new owners' differing hues, wall decorations, furnishings and illumination, but the kitchen is what it is. Aside from countertop accessories and the relatively minor decorating of the limited wall space, the room they see now is essentially the kitchen they will live with.

Encourage an attractive, clean area, brightened with a human touch that is carried through into the dinette area—a table with placemats and a spray of flowers is a welcoming sight. And yes, if the magnet still works on the refrigerator door, a postcard from a friend in Acapulco and a Garfield diet cartoon are OK—it's still the owners' home to enjoy!

*   *   *   *

Having insured that a human family, who are neither curators nor Sanford and Son, inhabit the home, glance around the yard. View the patio as an outdoor extension of the home and suggest the same aura—not messy and cluttered, yet casual enough to make the visitor want to go outside and sunbathe or play catch. A warning: Patios and decks are excellent repositories for illogical odds and ends. Strive for a few chairs, a chaise, the barbecue, a picnic table and a side table or two. Redwood planter tubs are nice. But garden equipment, bikes, firewood and other inappropriate clutter diminish the apparent expanse of the area.

Finally, trek out to the garage, the underlying function of which is to enclose a car or two. First and foremost, determine that at least twenty feet are available from the main door(s) to any permanent obstruction, such as a workbench or shelving. At the risk of brooking an element of chauvinism, our experience has been that a commodious or at least uncluttered garage is as important a selling feature to the male buyer as the kitchen usually is to his bride. As a room, it's the stepchild of the home it adjoins, but never underestimate the garage as an amenity of the home to a buyer, and encourage a modicum of order out there.

*   *   *   *

By now you have spent not a small amount of time counseling your client on arrangement and quantity of personal property—the dichotomy is that you're not even being paid to sell the stuff, but so long as the home is being shown while occupied and furnished by the owner, the thrust of the discussion in these chapters is integral to the effort. Distinguish your listing from others by taking advantage of the owners' more attractive possessions to create a natural, inviting atmosphere during a visit by the buyer.

These past three chapters have enabled us to put the home and the owners' property in the most advantageous light—the duty they charged us with. Note the entirety of the emphasis thus far has involved the interaction of only two parties to the sale—the listing agent and the seller. We've arrived at a point in the chronology of the transaction where others will soon become involved in the marketing process—the cobrokers and the eventual buyers.

Ideally for us, although not of particular concern to the seller, we might now bring our own buyer. (On the surface this is our dream come true, and it will receive more attention in the Offer chapter.)

Statistically, however, we will not make the sale alone, but will be assisted by another agent. And the stats lean toward the eventuality that the other agent will be from another office. (Those latter predictions are valid in our area, possibly not in yours.)

With that probability in mind, the next chapter will encourage a high degree of cooperation and communication with the other, as yet unknown, agent who will soon show your new listing. Our tips, for the most part, will benefit you even if you are showing and selling the listing unassisted.

Now don't give up—we'll get a real live buyer into the home soon, but we're still not quite ready....

"Minor rearrangement of personal property is occasionally required."

10

Coordination + Cooperation = Commission

One bright day a few years ago, a friend drove his three clients a half-hour south of our town to look at a home. The key in the lockbox wouldn't fit the door.

He then did what any trained professional would have done: He removed the lockbox from the doorknob and used it to beat a hole in the glass next to the front door—yet another novel use for a lockbox.

Gingerly reaching through the new aperture in the entry, he opened the door wide and invited his clients to join him inside. He sold the home.

In this chapter, we'd like to delve into a more urbane approach to selling real estate.

*   *   *   *

Somewhere back in the preface, we promised to share some of the little magic about our chosen craft that would have been nice to know in the weeks that followed our first listing appointment. Some thoughts are coming up now.

Several techniques are suggested with the assumption in mind that you are already developing a rapport with your fellow, but competing, agents in your market area. For as we said, your most formidable competitor at nine o'clock any morning just may become your closest, albeit short-term, ally by noon.

At this very moment, she may be taking a call from a prospect, looking for a home exactly like your new listing. Maybe yours and two others like it are on the market. Owing to your pleasant, upbeat profile and participation with her in a recent civic function—and the lower visibility of the other two listing agents—you get the first call for an appointment. Your outgoing attitude proved to be the first step in selling a home.

You've now been given a chance to do more than set up an appointment—your office secretary could do that. What you've earned for your visibility is the chance to talk with the showing agent and arm her with supplemental information about the listing. In the next few pages we'll see a few leads that will help her to write an offer on the home.

* * * *

We never cease to be amazed at the number of homes that are shown at the wrong time of the day! Any twenty-four-hour period is more than darkness followed by daylight, then a return to the dark. We pity those who don't comprehend the subtle beauty of dawn changing to morning, to afternoon, followed by sunset, shadowless dusk, then nightfall. Many of our compadres manage their leisure time within a dictum of the optimum time to see the spin on a tennis ball, flycast on a river, or view the sun setting behind the spinnaker of a Cal-20, running downwind to berth for the evening.

Unfortunately, the same agent who marvels as the sun disappears into the Pacific behind Santa Catalina doesn't quite get it together to tell us that he's listed a home with dramatic clerestory, Cape Cod or stained glass windows that look really nifty after three o'clock in the afternoon, or that the master bedroom is dark in midday, but great before noon.

The message: There's an advantageous time to visit any home, a time when it is the brightest inside and overall looks its best. A corollary: Every home has an exposure or layout when its interior is the darkest. Analyse your new listing—what's the best feature, room, area, view—and what time of the day does that feature fairly reach out and take a prospect by her ballpoint hand, reducing her to putty in yours?

THAT'S when you show the home or, within the context of this chapter, when you encourage your cobroker to bring her buyer. We get a little assertive when time is involved—both with the seller and the cobroker. In the absence of some genuinely restrictive time constraint, we shoot for the best time to see the home's amenities, not necessarily the most convenient for the buyer, cobroker or owner. That's called *selling a home*, which is what we're paid to do.

*   *   *   *

When showing a home with a dynamite view of a populated area, like many in our town that are built on the hills above the city with a view corridor to the downtown area:

We alluded to assertiveness and a showing like this will test your powers of persuasion. It's not difficult to set up—all that's necessary is to convince the owners to clean up the place and vacate over the dinner hour. Buy them a bucket of chicken if you have to, but run them out.

Then convince the cobroker, who's been showing homes all day, to look at one more during her dinner hour. The buyers will be equally pleased to give up their cocktail by the motel pool to see the house on the hill.

We promise that if you've done your homework and prepared the house, the effort will be productive. They first see the home in natural light—the full impact of the landscaping, the color and texture of the structure itself, the surrounding neighborhood and landmarks in the daylight view. While you chat, Mother Nature turns down the lights and the home and view take on the soft character of night, with distant landmarks defined by streetlights and other nighttime illumination. Even the interior of the home changes as the daylit home the buyers entered segues into the peaceful essence of evening.

Using this presunset technique, the sum of the showing will exceed the parts. A daylight appointment followed by another during the evening would have fallen short of demonstrating the transition from day to dark, a pleasure the prospects will be blessed to enjoy 365 times a year after they buy the home.

The cobroker who was ready to slaughter you for demanding a dinner-hour showing will sing praises of your wisdom for all to hear, right after she writes the offer for the star-struck buyers.

*   *   *   *

Analyzing your listing's optimum showing time, part two: Notwithstanding the paragraph above, here's a second reason for being a little assertive about when the listing is available for tour by clamoring buyers. Consideration must be given to external influences taking place on a recurring basis in the vicinity of the home that might have an adverse effect on the first impressions. Showing should be dovetailed around those influences.

A necessity: Spend a little time in the neighborhood, getting your finger on the pulse of what happens during the day.

At the head of the list, a school in the proximity is an impact to weigh. Schools usually get out around three o'clock in our area, and for this reason we would be disinclined to show a home in the traffic pattern of a school for an hour after that time. Schools generate traffic, be it parents picking up or delivering or the little tykes themselves, grown tall and strong and capable of operating their own cars. Our experience is that a middle school or junior high in the vicinity is the least bothersome from a marketing standpoint. The student body as a whole is too old to be seen with mom or dad, too young to drive and seems content to merely pedal or shuffle around the area.

Examples flow outward from schools. Obviously, any arterial street bearing a lot of traffic during some hour of the day should be considered. Parks and playgrounds are a major amenity to a neighborhood, but some host youth or adult sports leagues, with attendant traffic, PA systems and field lighting well into the evening. Show the home for the first time when the park use is minimal.

Our favorite personal example was a condominium we listed a few years ago in an area not far from the end of the main runway of our local airport. Airliners bent around to the east after takeoff and posed little noise problem. Harder to ignore were our Air Guard's RF-4C "Phantoms," venerable warbirds that pilots offer as proof positive that if enough power were hooked to a boxcar, it too could fly. We very soon learned that the Guard flew several defined afternoons each week and every fourth weekend. Guess when the condo wasn't shown. . . .

*   *   *   *

While we offer some examples in fun, we should roar out a serious aspect of time preference for showings as loudly as two Phantoms on tandem-takeoff:

The ethical consideration is this: We don't advocate managing the prospects' visits to any home to the hours that we alone select, in hopes of closing the escrow just before the 124-team Sertoma Softball League throws out the first pitch of a two-week night tournament being waged across the street. Read it here and heed: The totality of the listing and the neighborhood, the bitter and the sweet, must be demonstrated to a buyer. We are ethically comfortable, however, with an initial showing time that presents the fewest foreseeable distractions.

*   *   *   *

Departing now from time of showing, another category of information that ideally you will have an opportunity to convey to your cobroker when she calls for a showing appointment is the preferred route to follow to the listing.

Several facets of this route advisory are important. First, it should be the route least confusing to the buyer—many buyers prefer to meet their agent, driving their own car. (We've known buyers who felt "hostage" when we drove them.) Secondly, if there is an option, the chosen route should pass the largest number of attractive plusses or, restated, the fewest drawbacks. Finally, the path chosen should bring the buyers up to the home from the side with the better exposure. Most listings, like a human countenance, have a good side and a better side.

Putting aside the good versus inferior in the listing or the neighborhood, many of our listings are just plain hard to find, particularly in oddball subdivisions or hilly terrain areas, with short terraced streets and culs-de-sac. If your listing falls within this category, be prepared to offer better-than-usual directions and landmarks to your cobroker or prospect.

*   *   *   *

During each person's career some hurdles will be met and some mountains must be scaled. Your Mt. Everest may well be the phone call that mentions "The key you gave me wouldn't work"; Kilimanjaro is "The lockbox was empty." The fun one, the true Matterhorn at Disneyland is "The neighborhood is very safe; the police only took two minutes to get here." (We know all about that one—we once had the opportunity to discuss a listing in depth with our clients with all of our palms flat on the hood of a patrol car while Reno's Finest checked out a seller-broker relationship—mine.)

A lot of trouble has been taken to make the listing look good: The sellers have been primed to cooperate and the cobroker and buyer are present by our route at a beneficial time. Let's make sure they get inside the home, where we've staged this matinee.

We'll preface the whole access discussion with a personal belief: We hold that the listing agent should try to be present at each showing of her own listing. After all, who knows the home better—who knows the dog's name, the location of the light switch at the basement stairwell, and the owner's preference for financing, close date or what furniture is available. And she can broaden her own knowledge with each visit.

When the listing agent is present during a majority of showings, she is able to witness firsthand a variety of buyers' reactions to the home, then fine-tune any drawbacks in time for future prospect visits. Were she content to wait in her office while her listing was shown, she could only hope that the selling agents would give her an accurate representation of buyers' objections.

Ideally, the listing agent, arriving ahead of the cobroker and client, can get the house open, nullifying the house-key language that follows in the next few paragraphs. She can turn on the lights in dark rooms, open the drapes, fire up the stereo and hide the kids' skippers that didn't make it into the hamper that morning. In general, she can fine-tune the showing then be available or in hiding upon the preference of the showing cobroker. Our own preference is that the listing agent be available to help with questions that we have no way of answering during our first visit to her listing.

The reality: Part of a national park in the Black Hills of South Dakota is being dedicated as a resting place for those brokers who advocate the listing-broker-present theory, alongside all the other dinosaurs of North America. The pendulum has swung the other way—we were recently told by an affiliate of a youngish office that their marketing policy mandated that we could not be on the premises during the showing of one of our own listings by their agent. An interesting policy . . .

OK—so you want to visit our listing—we'll get you in.

*   *   *   *

Discounting the proven fact that three out of four homes in America have a key hidden either on top of the porchlight or under a flower pot on the step, we'll rely on the usual and legal methods of permissive entry.

The simplest is to call the owner to say a prospect will be enroute. The call is mandatory in some cases, and we think always a courtesy, even when the owner tells you to show it anytime you want. "We're always ready," say they—believe us, they're not. The mark of a truly seasoned veteran is the dexterity with which he can point out unique features of the listing with one hand and offer the seller a towel with the other, as she bolts out of the shower. Call ahead, unless you know for sure the owners are in the south of France or further from home.

If the owner is willing to provide access and then depart for a while, have a meeting of the minds in regard to relocking and securing the home. Offer him the showing agent's name and office and indicate a time of arrival reasonably within a half-hour period. We hope that you told the owner during the early stages of the listing process to defer inquiries about the marketing to you and to resist even the most innocuous questions from the cobroker or buyer.

*   *   *   *

On the score of innocuous questions, we've been shuffling a note card around looking for a place to insert it, and this might be the place. Innocuous question: "What are the utility bills?"

Imagine two families living side by side in two identical homes: Family A, a husband and wife with two small children, do their laundry at home, eat at home every night, leave home one week a year on vacation and heat or air-condition the place every day to 70°, summer and winter. She is artistic and makes pottery, firing her work in her own 220-volt, 5000-watt kiln in the garage. He is less creative, but does relax in the evening with his arc-welder.

Family B, two empty-nesters, enjoy their motor home a good part of the year and dine out frequently when they are in town. She hates air-conditioning, they both like their wood-burning stove and they send their laundry out.

The point: Utility bills are an oft-discussed issue and are about as relevant to the transaction as the buyer asking the seller how much gas she burns in her Pontiac wagon each year. Unless you're dealing with clients with the exact lifestyle as the homeseller, a comparison is valueless and is best avoided.

*   *   *   *

In the owner's absence from the home, a key may be picked up at your office or other agreeable location. We discourage the old key-with-the-neighbor trick, after having seen lost keys and misunderstood instructions, neighbors "helping" the cobroker show the home or this real dandy that occurred in our town: A well-meaning neighbor played salesperson, showing the listed home to all and sundry who slowed down in front of the For Sale sign. Exceptional behavior, admittedly, but who needs it?

Mark the key with your office name and a code to identify the listing address on the key. While the reason for this seems elementary, we still pick up keys all the time with the address boldly marked on the key tag. We take the custody of a key very seriously—very early in our career, a coworker misplaced the key to a home with five exterior doors with Schlage locks and deadbolts keyed alike. The goof cost over $200 then to recylinder all the locksets and would cost plenty more now. No amount of money could cure the unprofessional and careless impression that the mistake created.

Finally—log keys out to cobrokers and pursue their timely return. Two reasons dictate this effort—first, the longer a key stays out the more it starts looking like every other key in the cobroker's purse, tagged or not. They have a way of going into a pit somewhere below the earth that now contains about a zillion house keys—all tagged. (The same pit, by the way, that single socks go in when they leave the dryer.)

The second and arguably the more important motivation for chasing keys down is that a key riding around in somebody's glove box does you no good when the next agent, possibly with a dead-cinch buyer, needs access to your listing. For want of a key . . . you know the rest.

*   *   *   *

Lockboxes are quite prevalent in our business. The uninitiated are entitled to a short description of these devices: A sturdy box, about the size of a pocket pager, with a shank on one end to attach the box to a doorknob or other protrusion on the listing. Licensees who belong to a local trade association sponsoring the system are issued a key, that opens all that association's boxes. The listing agent places a door key for the listing in the lockbox and attaches the box to the home. Other agents may then use their own lockbox key to open the box, remove the listing's key, and show the home—spared the time necessary to run about town picking up and returning keys to the listing offices.

Technology ranges from a simple keyed box, upward to units requiring a combination code in conjunction with a key, or boxes that imprint individual agent's codes on a foil tape, creating a record of who showed the listing.

*   *   *   *

Whatever type of lockbox prevails in your area, make sure that your listing's box is convenient, if you are using that method of access. The front door knob is almost too inviting—we like a gas meter or decorative iron work or other protrusions close to the front door but well-hidden enough to be concealed from view from the street. It should be reasonably accessible to agents, and clear of pyracantha bushes or mud puddles.

Check in the listing's own locks whatever keys you give to other agents. Many older homes have worn keyways on the locksets and the owner's key may well be as worn as the locks. Together they work well, but a new duplicate key cut from the worn key may not turn. Schlage is famous (or notorious!) for close tolerances in tumblers, and duplicates must almost always be cut from an original key to work easily. (If Schlage reads this, we hope they take it as a compliment to their quality.)

Finally, if you're using a lockbox, enlist the owner's help in glancing at it once in a while, to ensure that the lid's in place or that it otherwise appears serviceable.

*   *   *   *

Alarms pose unique problems and are becoming a more prevalent system to contend with than they were a few years ago. Our office has a firm policy about alarms: If the owner isn't there to secure the thing, then we will be. The last thing we need to be responsible for is to divulge the code to another agent. The obverse also holds true—we don't want the alarm code for your listing. If the place gets burgled while the alarm was silenced, our ignorance is our bliss. Know the alarm company's phone number—if you do set it off, you might have a chance to head off the gendarmes with a phone call if the alarm hasn't already captured the telephone line.

If the alarm in the home has a panic button feature, usually found in the bedroom and kitchen, it may be plain and unobtrusive or may be marked *Emergency*. Prospects have a delightful propensity for pushing buttons and the best way to insure a poke is to mark a button: *Emergency*. That invitation ranks right up with a sign indicating *Wet Paint*. Keep an eye on that button when proximate to it with visitors— we thought once that we had the only buyer west of the Mississippi goofy enough to push a silent alarm button and roll the police, until an alarm company salesperson revealed that homes for sale account for more false alarms than any other cause.

Two last words about alarms—one, recall the listing chapter and determine ownership of the system—it may be only leased. Finally, we help the new owners with many details, but let them coordinate with the alarm company privately about recoding the system. We don't want to know anything about it. In the same vein, we encourage new owners to rekey the exterior locks. The former owner usually has let keys out to friends, neighbors, housekeepers and babysitters, and a marketing effort widens the margin for a lost or feloniously retained key. Advise them to start fresh.

*   *   *   *

Your clients' safety, and indeed your own, deserves a brief mention. We'll include three of the most prevalent liability exposures and hope that you look about the listing and anticipate others, should there be any.

The first is one that you in the sunny southern climes can disregard and those of us who show and sell closer to the North Pole can fret about: snow and ice accumulation on the driveways, patios and walkways your clients must traverse. We put the responsibility squarely on the seller's shoulders during the listing appointment. Indeed, she owes safe passage not only to your clients, but her own family, friends, mailcarriers and others who visit her home.

Obviously, if the listing is vacant or the owner is out of town, somebody has to do the shoveling and salting after a storm—we leave the "who" to your resources, but urge that it be done before any prospects arrive.

A second hazard is more prevalent where the ice isn't—listings with swimming pools. A friend was once showing a client a home and heard a muffled splash. A quick head count revealed the entourage to be one kid short, and our friend, plucky lass that she is, dove in and retrieved the client's two-year-old from the deep end of the pool, then finished showing the home, still soaking wet. We recall the event now with humor, but the showing very nearly ended in tragedy.

*   *   *   *

The final danger enumerated here is the pet, usually canine, but not necessarily. We discovered one afternoon the power in a parrot's beak and learned later that El Papagayo well could have separated us from our offer-writing digit had he been a little more vigorous. (Is it 325° per hour per four pounds, and baste frequently? It works just right for a turkey....)

Typically, and seriously, the ubiquitous dog is a formidable problem. We've never been bitten by a vicious dog, only by four or five "playful" ones. If we're showing your listing, don't tell us his name is Freeway and he's OK if we call him by name—get him out of here. He makes the clients nervous and distracts our efforts to sell your listing. If you store him in a room during the showing, mark the room to remind us, because chances are good we'll forget unless he's barking. And if the situation can't be dealt with reliably, insist on the seller's presence during a showing.

Our client visits any listing as a contractual guest and we are charged with the duty of reasonable protection of her frame and hide, as is the seller. We can debate with the insurance adjustors and attorneys all day over primary liability of homeowner or broker in the case of an injury, but the bottom line is that we're trying to sell a house and an injured client is not what we need. Treat her like you'd treat any other friend—keep her from getting hurt in the first place.

*   *   *   *

The final suggestion for preparing the cobroker for a successful showing is what retailers call *point-of-sale motivators*, found around checkout lines in supermarkets. We call them brochures or fliers, left in a prominent location within the listing for removal by the buyer.

The cobroker touring the home with clients may only be prepared with a Multiple-Listing book that contains only basic information, and he may be silent as to the home's many amenities. Remember what we're trying to accomplish—to set the house apart from other candidates the prospect will visit, most of which are in the MLS® book in a format identical to yours. The fliers, kept available in a businesslike but inexpensive clear plastic holder by the front door, give your seller a memory-jogging edge, honed sharper with every other home the buyer sees. (Even experienced salespeople start losing track of features when too many similar homes are seen during a full day of home showing.)

The flier format may range from an inexpensive but well-prepared photocopied sheet that clearly describes the home and yard in detail with relevant information that you find positive, to a professionally produced effort including photographs. They serve the same purpose—they provide prospects with a souvenir of the visit.

It's a safe assumption that the buyers have looked at a fair number of homes in a short time period. We can think of little worse than having them love your listing, but be unable to identify it as their first choice. For this reason, we highlight the most memorable feature of the home. Recalling a recent chapter, attention to the home filled with choo-choo trains would be in order if that's the best we can do.

When the buyers are sitting around their motel pool, where all buyers go after a day of home-shopping, your listing will be the most vivid. And you'll probably be one of the few that supplied them with a flier—the practice is frequently forgotten.

Then the pièce de résistance for the flier: Include a map of the area, sufficient to beam the buyers in from some landmark in this strange new city back to the home.

Buyers have a propensity for driving past candidate homes after dinner, in the privacy afforded sans agent. Sometimes they like to "relook" at a neighborhood or see the character of the home during the evening. (Did we mention somewhere earlier that the seller should be encouraged to leave the porchlight on during the early evening while the home is on the market to add a little life to the home and yard and make the house number easier to read? We meant to.)

Accommodate the poolside prospects—give them a good map, right on the flier. It may be the only map to a listing they were given all day, and the only listing they can retour that evening. Your phone may ring early the next morn or even later the same night with a pair of excited buyers on the other end of the line.

*   *   *   *

Open Houses

It's a Sunday afternoon in All-America Town, USA. But it's not Mother's Day, Father's Day, Easter or a Sunday in December and it's definitely not Super Bowl Sunday. The aroma of turkey and dressing doesn't permeate the air—not much happens after Thanksgiving, Pilgrim.

Hopefully, it's not the first sunny Sunday after a gloomy spring, when the citizenry is out for the first time mulching their violets and trying for a tan line.

We've run an ad in the paper telling all of our hospitality, convinced the owners to go wherever owners go during open houses, and we've put a sign out front and a few signs with arrows down by the arterial streets. The home is squeaky clean, we've brought a bag of munchies and we've run off a handful of fliers.

An open house is happening—the Woodstock of suburbia, a singularly American event rivaled in popularity only by a garage sale. (Historians will prove that Americans visited strangers' garages on Saturdays and returned on Sundays to see each other's homes.)

*   *   *   *

A visit by a prospect to an open house differs immensely from the visit by appointment. During the latter, the buyers' identity is known, their ability to purchase has been assessed by a licensee and their relationship with an agent is declared.

Compare that to an open house situation, where we meet a great many Mr. Smiths and Mrs. Joneses, few of whom ever divulge their allegiance to the proverbial Broker B immortalized in our textbooks.

*   *   *   *

The peril we're steering you toward is a monumental problem in procuring cause—the doctrine defining the licensee who in fact, is, to be credited with motivating a buyer to buy and thereby the agent entitled to be compensated for those efforts. Procuring cause disputes are not tabulated on a nationwide basis like Major League batting averages, but we'd bet that in a vast majority of these disputes, an open house was at the headwaters of the ensuing river of grief.

Frequently the licensee is not at fault. We tell our prospects to call us when they find a home they'd like to visit. Forget it. They see a dollhouse with a view, open on a Sunday afternoon with three prospects' cars parked in front, and they panic. The dollhouse will be gone tomorrow morn if they don't go inside and get the ball rolling.

The agent within, unaware of their relationship with you, shows them the home, lines up financing possibilities and, in short, spends a great deal of time with them. (And misses a chance to talk to another viable couple in the home.)

You, similarly unaware of your prospects' activities, get a call Monday morning. The prospects dictate the offer to write up, chapter and verse, down to financing and personal property to be included.

Regrettably, agents occasionally comply with the prospects' wishes. In depth:

A cardinal rule in our business is that you *never sell a home you haven't visited with the buyers.* Some say it's a written law, but most agents agree it's just good sense. (We once showed a couple a home that they had been occupying as tenants for five years—they knew the place better than we did or the landlord did, but as the situation changed from rental to ownership, visit it we must.)

The second reason for not writing such an offer is that you didn't do anything to earn a commission. The listing agent's advertising drew the buyers to the home and her time spent with them motivated them to buy this house and not another. She will no doubt point that out to you as your offer arrives on her desk.

Assuming she is ethical, she will work to the benefit of the seller by presenting your offer, leaving the acrimony between agents out of the process. If a conveyance results, rest assured that the commission distribution between agents will be disputed and she's an odds-on favorite to prevail.

Which is different than winning—in these matters there are no winners. The brokerage system, however, loses.

*   *   *   *

Now, a better way to approach these situations: Some would say, tell the prospects not to look at any homes without you in tow. That won't happen—our prospects are responsible citizens six days a week; on the Sabbath, their minds click into idle and an open house draws them like moths to flames.

Some agents give buyers their business cards in quantity to present to agents at open houses, as a signal that they are another salesperson's prospect. That's a nice melodramatic touch, but veteran agents are a little skittish about having their cards floating all over town indiscriminately. (Cards with the agent's picture aren't a bad idea in this business.)

An acceptable compromise is to implore our buyers to disclose to the host agent, at the instant that their Reeboks hit the front stoop, that they are working with Karl Breckenridge and will call upon him to assist in their purchase of the home if they make that decision.

This allows the agent to let them see the home and extend them courtesy, but saves the nitty-gritty details and bottom-line insights for the licensed person who will likely become the selling agent. This practice seems to be the trend across America in addressing an intricate *procuring cause* and client-education dilemma.

*   *   *   *

In a concurrent vein, see if this thought finds acceptance in your market area: If you are working with a rogue prospect, sure to spend his time touring other agents' open houses, give him a list of those homes that are candidates for his needs. We personally hate this brand of marketing and feel like we're doing less than our job, but if he's bound to go a-touring at his own pace and convenience, at least zero him in on the probables.

Then call the agents hosting the open houses you suggested, and inform (or warn) them that you're working with the guy in the red Ferrari with six pencils in his breast pocket, and give them all the aliases he's gravitated to recently. Most agents will extend him courtesy, but not be surprised when you enter the scene Monday morning.

We're in a backscratching business. We're happy to show your prospect our listing, so long as we know of your alliance with her. And we know you'll do the same for us another day. We're all entitled to a Sunday off once in a while with impunity.

But don't overwork this welcome—most agents take umbrage with salespeople who spend 49 Sundays a year enjoying the suds and surf at Main Beach in Laguna, while the rest of us are showing their prospects our listings.

*   *   *   *

We'll stay with the open house discussion for a few more pages, as these thoughts are relevant and too often learned the hard way.

A question forms the focus of the next few paragraphs: If you're the analytical sort, name a member of any other profession who is granted as high a degree of care, custody and control of the property of another as we are granted in the real estate profession on an almost daily basis. We have friends who get squirrelly leaving their $18,000 Prelude with a parking valet, who sweat bullets during the whole week that their $3,200 signed lithograph is in the frame shop and who won't take a silk blouse to one dry cleaner reputed to be the Bermuda Triangle of clothing. These same friends hand over the keys to their $250,000 + home, stacked to the rafters with valuable property, to a real estate agent—and they do it without a second thought.

*   *   *   *

A few pointers follow about the security of the owners' property during open houses:

The hazards are not unique to open houses, any more than any other client visit, save for the simple fact that open houses frequently (and hopefully) cause a larger number of people to be traversing the home at any given time. We owe it to our sellers to ensure that nothing is disturbed.

A point should be made to bring the following text into perspective: We're not all that worried about property being removed by buyers. In talking to other brokers around the country, we've found a consensus that theft during open houses or any other client visit is just not a significant problem. Prospects as a group are pretty good eggs.

What we are trying to stress is the possibility that some of the owner's property or the home itself may be tampered with, readjusted or otherwise toyed with, causing damage to the property or inconvenience to the owner.

As the complexity of the home grows, so grows the number of neat dials, switches and delicate personal property. We mentioned the silent-alarm panic button (pushed during an open house); we could mention a litany of complaints from owners about readjusted VCRs, stereo components, PCs and so on.

On a lighter note, we'll recall the best-publicized open house in our town, the one where the Reno Fire Department extricated a young lady from the laundry chute after her brother consigned her down for a gentle rinse and fluff dry.

Those big red trucks do draw a crowd. . . .

*   *   *   *

We minimize theft discussion, as we've never been impacted by a problem during our career. But we're not insensitive to the hazard. Usually common sense is all that we need to employ.

Veteran agents "sweep" a house prior to a showing or an open house, and find that owners are quite blasé about their property. One day we noted a gold Rolex watch atop the dresser, ripe for the pluckin', and put it into a drawer. That was smart. (Telling the seller where we put it would have been even smarter.)

Heighten the sellers' awareness of the security of their property so that they may share this rather awesome burden with you as you market the home.

The final note on security: When an overwhelming presence of high-value personal property is impossible or impractical to conceal during an open house, we Just Say No. We trust the homebuying public and like them all, but we're not naive, either. A few years ago a friend listed a home owned by a gun collector who was insistent about holding an open house. Our friend, assessing a display of ordnance sufficient to recreate the Alamo, declined. The seller fired him and found another agent. That agent held an open house and the home was broken into two weeks later.

While it would be a gross injustice to the profession and to the homebuying public to draw an absolute cause-and-effect link between the two events, most veterans would just as soon not even take the chance of precipitating such an occurrence.

* * * *

The buyers are on their way, and in the next chapter we'll give them the tour, but we have time for one quick note to wrap up the open-house segment. The note is about your own security during an open house in a secluded or out-of-the-way listing or during an evening showing that may conclude after dark. Many offices have a policy about these situations, but don't wait to be told. The message, in an upbeat vein, is that sometimes it's just nice to have a little company on appointments—take another agent along.

Well, imagine our surprise. The buyers are on the doorstep, impressed by the path through the neighborhood, the sun is glinting through the stained glass in the entry, the bases are empty on the softball diamond across the park, nary a car moves on the street and the key slides into the lockset and clicks a quarter-turn to the right. No alarms, no Dobermans—we're ready to sell a house.

11

Showtime!

*Wise agents learn very early that we can't sell a home through pres-
sure and duress and expect the transaction to hold together.*

*What we can do is show a qualified buyer every benefit and amen-
ity of ownership, as well as the inherent drawbacks that every listing
incorporates.*

A home, properly marketed and shown, sells itself.

* * * *

No two salespeople show homes the same way, no two buyers react the
same to any one house and no two salespeople have an identical rapport with a buyer or perception of any given home.

Having now conclusively identified the similarities in home-
showing as being none whatsoever, we're free to roam about the chapter's thrust with almost no constraints or sequence. The underlying
intent is to convey a few techniques that work for successful veterans,
with the hope that some of them may be integrated into your showings
to your benefit.

Much of the chapter is written around the premise that buyers
tend to look at any home from the vantage point of how their guests
will view this home, should they pursue the purchase. Help them
make this mental transition by making them feel like guests in the listing. Whatever they might feel disposed to do in anticipation of company, you do for them.

The word *sequence*, appearing above, fades into oblivion through the next few pages. The thoughts conveyed now may be useful during any stage of the showing—suggestions to employ whenever the timing is most opportune.

Invite your guests to park in the driveway and enter through the front door. If the owners are at home, they are entitled to an introduction to agents and buyers.

Both parties will feel more comfortable and welcome. The continual reluctance of some agents to introduce visitors is perceived by many sellers as rude. And offer a business card, establishing with the seller that you are, in fact, a salesperson. (We advise our sellers to request a card if none is offered.)

Schools of thought vary about the route to follow through the home during a showing. One of two conditions prevail:

Some visitors are content with and even expect a guided tour on a route that you have preplanned as the most advantageous to maximize the impact of the home. By now, within your own listing, you should have determined that path and may now depart in that direction.

Other guests recognize no barriers. They came to see, and will charge off toward whatever amenity catches their eye first. So long as they stay reasonably grouped, most experienced agents don't resist that free roaming—the amenity they may be racing to inspect may be the one that ultimately sells the home. We'd be foolish to curtail their interest until that feature appears on our predetermined route. Some assertiveness may be necessary, however, to prevent having buyers spread hither and yon throughout the home.

A peril to recognize in the wild-and-free visits is that an area may be breached that buyers don't belong in, i.e., wet paint or dry German Shepherd or that a part of the home may be missed entirely.

Within this context, children accompanying buyers need some supervision. Our personal feeling is that the presence of the buyers' kids compromises the attention of both the agent and the buyers, but their presence is frequently a reality of home showing. In any case, protect the property of the seller from the children's curiosity.

Throughout the listing chapter many amenities crept into the enumeration of features. Little regard was assigned to quality; within that chapter, it mattered not—the amenity was there or it wasn't. As the emphasis now turns to showing the listing, quality acquires importance.

Short of droning on with endless patter more likely to irritate than elucidate, you should now highlight the quality features. The skill of "reading" the buyer is important here—some readily identify, unassisted, the quality features; others rely upon you to show them. Abandoning any sequence, let's help them along.

*   *   *   *

Common throughout the home: premium window units—Anderson, Pella, metal-clad wood sashes and mullions and reflective coatings on the afternoon side of the house. Sills: Formica-type, Coryon or ceramic tile—durable in harsh or wet climates. (Wood sills are acceptable in formal living and dining rooms.) Motorized drape pulls, sheer curtains, upgraded valances, Plantation or jalousie louvered shutters and Vertiblinds—the list goes on.

Point out noise-abatement and energy-saving qualities of dual-glazed windows, if your home is so equipped. (Quick test: Hold the tip of a key or ballpoint against the glass—dual windows create a double reflection, one a half-inch or so behind the other.)

Interior doors may be plusses—three hinges per door are prevalent in better homes (actually a pair and a half of hinges) panel or insert doors, louvered doors, French or Dutch doors. Hardware: Schlage, brass or any upgraded locksets. Specialized doors: self-closures, double swung or cafe doors, where desirable.

*   *   *   *

Watt we like in electricity (nothing shocking): logical switch locations in rooms, alternate switches in hallways and larger rooms, dimmers, time-clocks or photocells on exterior lights and automatic switches to shut off lights in little-used rooms after a reasonable period of time. Door-operated closet lights, switches available in outside locations for safety or security.

Grounded (three-prong) duplex plugs, plugs in several exterior locations for hedge trimmers and car vacuums, GFI (Ground-Fault Interruptor) plugs in water-prone areas (bathrooms, exterior). Overhead fixtures, always a premium in bedrooms (absent in the low-ceiling bedrooms prevalent a decade ago), coffered perimeter lighting, upgraded bathroom fixtures and recessed luminescent ceilings in kitchens.

On to heating and cooling systems (frequently called the *mechanical* systems): Chronotherm-type thermostats to reduce demand during the evenings, a furnace location away from the sleeping area (quiet), ditto the air-conditioner—never under the bedroom window! Owner-serviceable filters. A fast-recovery water heater, close to the service area. Constant-recirculating hot water is nice, but many systems were abandoned during the energy crunch a decade ago.

*   *   *   *

A brief mention of laundry rooms, an area second only to the kitchen in some buyers' priorities. Obviously, full plumbing hookups and drain for the washer; 220-volt power or gas bibb for the dryer and a dryer vent to the exterior, or at least to a place where hot air and condensation are acceptable. Storage is nice—in many newer homes the broom closet appears in the laundry or utility room. Requiring little preparation save for space is an area for sewing, ironing and folding clothes. Built-in ironing boards are nice, but many homeowners prefer a portable board. A bathroom-type ceiling fan can pull out dryer heat in the summer.

*   *   *   *

What's cooking in the kitchen: Large-format ceramic tile with contrasting grout seems to be the premium, but many buyers still prefer preformed Formica-type countertops and splashes. Divided sinks, a plus—sinks with a third basin for the disposer are top-drawer. Most buyers prefer self-rimming sinks to top-set types, for ease of cleaning and scooting debris off the counters. Single-handle mixing valves, rinsing hoses and instant hot-water taps (for soup, tea and coffee) are upgrades to call attention to. Water-softener or purifying units are desirable in many areas of the country. Modern homes without disposers are almost nonexistent—the better types have a separate switch instead of the older drainplug-operated switches.

Dishwashers, too, are almost standard. Look for the models with extra features and time-delayed starts. Get to know premium cooktops and ovens—down-venting ranges with a selection of cooking surfaces are premium, self-cleaning and convection ovens are tops. A good rangehood and light is an amenity, ditto a microwave included in the sale and a garbage compactor.

"Keep your client off the cooktop, she's too old to ride the range...."
—Revis M. Edwards, 1972

Point out quality cupboards and cabinets—lazy Susans in corner cabinets, adjustable shelves, Formica-inlaid shelf surfaces, glassware or specialized cookware racks, pull-out breadboards. Lots of plugs are nice, as is a wall-mount telephone jack and hanger.

Don't forget the refrigerator. Determine whether it's included in the sale and look for a plumbed ice-maker water supply.

Floor surface preferences vary. Coved baseboards are the Cadillac of premium homes, but losing out in new construction due to high installation-labor costs. Good-grade top-set vinyl base is gaining acceptance, as is the use of hardwood baseboard. Some buyers like carpet; others like random-plank flooring.

Finally in the kitchen—a sink without an exterior view renders the home harder to sell. A view into the adjoining room is a good compromise.

*　*　*　*

The last room to be specifically addressed is the bathroom. At random, a few popular amenities:

Interesting lighting fixtures, generous medicine and storage cabinets, swing-out, side-view makeup mirrors and attractive towel bars. A ventilating fan is nice, particularly if switched separately from the lights. Heat lamps are OK, wall heaters are OK if wired to an escapement switch so they don't accidentally stay on all day. Aluminum shower enclosures are better if anodized in a color other than mill (gray) finish. Frosted shower doors are easier to clean than clear glass.

Oversize and steeping (deep) tubs are definite upgrades: Jacuzzi or pump-type tubs are superior. Single-knob mixing valves are good in tubs and showers, as are pulsating and high shower heads. (Most showers are plumbed five feet, nine or five feet, ten inches high—great for Happy, Sleepy, Bashful and friends, but tough on the taller guys.) Ditto the high counter tops now coming into vogue. Floors? Preferences vary—look for quality, be it the carpet (usually removable), ceramic tile or linoleum. Older vinyl-asphaltic tile is a killer to keep clean.

A decade ago, single-handle valves in basins were popular but the trend is returning to attractive separate hot and cold controls, frequently with a matching fill spout and soap dishes, water-tumbler holders and mirrors. (To avoid disappointment, find out if the removable accessories stay or go, and represent them appropriately to the prospects.)

Single-unit (integral tank and bowl) toilets were popular for a time, but received a john-diced eye from builders and owners due to high shipping weight, complexity of repairs and the all-or-nothing replacement problem. They're nice, but not mandatory in an otherwise premium home. Silent-flush and vented models remain on the market and are clearly superior, worth noting if the listing is so equipped.

*   *   *   *

Other amenitites pop up almost everywhere in the home—with experience you will recognize what buyers enjoy seeing: textured and painted ceilings instead of blown-acoustic "popcorn" treatments (a no-no in a kitchen or bathroom!), windows on two separate walls in bedrooms, the hallmark of a prewar premium custom home. Little things mean a lot—Westminster door chimes, separate front-door and back-door bell tones, at least one hard-surface entry (usually close to the kitchen), at least one grade-level entry door. Copious telephone jacks, prewired stereo jacks and cable TV plugs. Watch the older central light switches and indicators, frequently in master bedrooms—if they're low voltage, they can be nightmares to repair. Fireplaces vary from simple places to burn splinters of wood to large 42-inch (or bigger) beauties, some with Heatilator-type ducts and electric fans. Large hearths and mantels are nice places to leave cookies for Santa. Airtight inserts and woodstoves are premium, but are also becoming a cause célèbre in many areas due to air quality controls. These bear investigation if your area is impacted by such legislation.

*   *   *   *

A valuable sales tool that's frequently overlooked by agents is the existence of covenants, conditions and restrictions (CC&R) and/or deed restrictions. Many buyers are pleased to learn that they will never have to look out the parlor window at the broadside of a class-A motorhome or that the neighbor next door is precluded from adding a second story that will doom the buyers to a lifetime of early afternoon sunsets.

CC&Rs and deed restrictions occasionally smoke out the "nobody's going to tell me what I can do with my house" genre of buyers. Upon hearing this proclamation, a wise agent can usually use the goose-versus-gander analogy—the rules bear not only on him but everyone else in the subdivision, and the total effect is a more attractive neighborhood and higher property values.

Be conversant in the rules and regs governing the listing and use them as effectively as any physical amenity of the home.

*   *   *   *

The exterior of the home also holds upgrades to tempt a buyer: better-grade exterior doors, locksets and deadbolts, preferably keyed alike. Raingutters and downspouts in good repair, voiding water into an area not likely to freeze or collect. Where raingutters don't appear over porches and patios, look for diverters, sometimes architecturally preferable. Nice porchlights and lampposts are a plus. Heavy wrought-iron screen security doors are a premium. Circular driveways and porte-cochere entries are tremendously popular; a great compromise is a driveway configured to allow a driver to enter a public street without having to back out onto it.

A subtle amenity: water, gas and power meters on the street side of the back fence—accessible by utility meter readers without the need to enter an enclosed yard through potentially locked gates.

Most upgrades in a yard speak for themselves more readily than those inside the home. Don't forget the surrounding homes as amenities to your listing if they enhance the desirability.

*   *   *   *

Right about here we all need a short breather—writing about this myriad of amenities tests our stamina.

There's a subtle overtone to that feigned exhaustion—if we, seated at the typewriter, and you, in your easy chair, are bogged down by all these features, fancy the fatigue of the prospects. Absorbing this much visual stimuli is not an easy task.

The message? Sit down. Invite the buyers to relax for a few minutes and digest what they've seen. This invitation to lounge, while a break for them, perpetuates the marketing effort. A home takes on a wholly new character from chair level. Bear in mind, they are looking at this home partially through their guests' eyes. Make these guests of yours comfortable for a few minutes.

Then give them some privacy. We go out and check the handbrake on the car or visit a neighbor over the back fence. Invite them to look at the entirety of the home again without you in tow. Rejoin them after a period of time and solicit questions that may have come up during their moments alone.

A danger zone exists in a double-teaming approach. We frequently have two agents within a home during a client visit: one, the listing agent, providing access, the other showing the home to prospects. A threat arises when two agents assume the selling posture, intentionally or unwittingly, and overwhelm the buyers.

Try the comprehensive guided tour, followed by a time of privacy for your prospects. It's worked for many experienced agents.

*   *   *   *

The following are random notes that didn't fit anywhere else in particular, but are worth sharing:

Note one: If we know we'll be listing a home in the future, we visit the home with our camera and take a few shots when the home looks attractive. In our area, late winter's bleakness makes the Russian Urals seem like a garden spot—not a great time to show a home.

Take pictures of the home under a blanket of snow, lit by Christmas lights, or during the summer with vibrant landscaping, or in autumn's changing colors. Save them, then put them on the fireplace mantel for the buyers to see—a promise of better, prettier times to come.

New topic: barking dogs. The neighbor's barking dogs. At the risk of sounding like a snake-oil salesman, we tell buyers with some authority when the neighbor's dog starts raising a ruckus as we walk out into the yard, that the dog probably won't bark after they buy the home and their voices become known to the dog.

This sounds like a line, but in reality, dogs do react to strange new voices more readily than ones with which they are familiar. Use your own yard as a test—in all probability your neighbor's pooch doesn't pay any attention to you and your family members, but might speak up when you have company. Once the hint of a threat diminishes, the barking usually stops.

Notable: When showing homes with another agent, we constantly see the other agent shutting off lights about one microsecond after the client walks out of a room, as if to indicate "one more room down, end of showing near." Consistent with our recommendation to turn the clients loose to retour the home is our suggestion that you forget the lights—get them later. If you're on a roll, stay with the prospects out the door and all the way back to the office to write an offer.

* * * *

Next we address premeditated ignorance and a willingness on your part to say something less than charitable about the listing.

At some point during the showing we are usually asked a question for which we don't have an answer. (Or there is no answer or no meaningful answer, but the client nevertheless wants to know.) This situation represents a beautiful opportunity to turn ignorance to our favor. We admit we don't know, establishing ourselves as human and fallible, then we promise a response, affording an opportunity to demonstrate our deep sense of perseverance and professionalism. (The real opportunity is to have reason to call back for a follow-up on the showing appointment.)

The second act, the uncharitable comment, also defies some of our associates' sensibilities. The plain truth might be that the wallpaper is flat ugly and should be replaced. Admit it—agree wholeheartedly. Then have the estimate handy. The advantage: A spirit of candor is established with the prospects—they know that you're willing to address the bitter with the sweet, and every home has a little bitter. We're a little careful, however, and let the guests take the initiative to express their dislikes first. We very nearly rapped the bathroom fixtures in an otherwise exquisite home we showed a couple several years ago. The fixtures (matching tub, basins and WC) were the most unappealing purple-puce that Kohler ever cast during the adventurous-color era of the mid-fifties.

The buyer absolutely loved them—her parents had the same color in their custom home and she hadn't seen them in any other home she had ever visited. (We weren't surprised.) They bought the place, due in large part to the bathroom hues.

We should have been tipped off when they drove up to the listing in a pink, white and charcoal '56 DeSoto.

*   *   *   *

Confessing now that the DeSoto is a slight editorial enhancement for levity's sake, we'll start to let the prospects excuse themselves from the home temporarily, firmly intent on becoming the new owners soon.

Point-of-sale fliers should be offered and your business card should be in some conspicuous place to confirm to the owner that the home was visited.

If the owners were present during the showing, normal courtesy should be paid them upon your departure. If the home is unoccupied, security becomes paramount to marketing for a few moments. Secure the lights and locks—make sure the lockbox key gets back into the box.

We like to leave the impression with the prospects that they are welcome to an encore. Frequently, clients visiting a complex home want to see the home again to refresh their memory—we make that invitation for a retour.

*   *   *   *

Early in the chapter we predicted that no two homes, agents or prospects are ever the same, and now we reiterate that thought. We have in these pages witnessed only the tip of the home-showing iceberg—our intent is to create a skeletal basis for your experience to grow from and we leave it to you to look around the homes you show and "flesh in" that skeleton.

A brief review of our path thus far: We've listed a home correctly and prepared it well for viewing. It's been visited by a qualified client whom you've made totally conversant with the benefits and drawbacks of owning this home. We're now at the threshhold of a lengthy but productive chapter—soon we are going to tell the seller what the buyer will offer to purchase the home and what the seller will convey to the buyer in return for that consideration. Obligations will be contractually created and a time schedule will be established, binding upon all the parties to the transaction, yourself included. This form, like the *listing contract*, is the document that brings successful sales to fruition.

12

The Dotted Line

If a reader came west and visited one of our homes, it's quite possible she might see a sign over the front door: "Mi casa es su casa." Many of us have adopted that greeting from the Spaniards who first settled our land—the words translate to "My house is your house."

We of the real estate profession embrace this lovely and welcoming sentiment and embellish it slightly, by adding a six-figure price, to make sure that the sellers' house truly becomes the buyers' house.

For our efforts, we try to channel a little dinero down the arroyo our way, to keep our own haciendas running.

*   *   *   *

Prior to embarking on this discussion of the offer, we should recollect a few thoughts contained in the preamble to the listing chapter, as those thoughts are quite relevant here also.

The initial echo is the statement of intent of this book: an overview for beginners to be used in conjunction with other texts and material supplied by your office training program. An in-depth dissection of any offer demands a knowledge of specific listing information, known buyers and sellers, in a finite financing environment. A comprehensive discussion without these pieces of the puzzle would be counterproductive.

What we'll soon discuss is a generalized look at language contained in virtually all offer contracts.

Just as we used a typical listing form earlier, this chapter assumes that we have now a standard, state-approved offer form—possibly revised to suit the needs of a particular brokerage office, but containing the elements essential to legality. As we move through the form, you should recognize the intent and wording, if not the exact sequence, of their appearance.

We took the stance in the listing chapter that the listing price determination fell outside the discipline of this book—in reality, a function of localized appraisal techniques combined with experienced, case-basis help from your manager. Within the quick-start mission of this book, we deferred that discussion to appraisal texts and resources as applied to a known, specific listing of your own. Here in this chapter, we continue that premise—offering price itself is not integrated into the text.

The form before us is probably captioned "Purchase agreement and deposit receipt." The deposit receipt segment of that form is worthy of significant attention. It starts, "Received from _____."

"Received from" is not always synonymous with "who's buying the house." We'll offer three prevalent examples:

1. An individual deposits earnest money to purchase a home for himself and his intended spouse. In fact, they plan to be married prior to recordation of the deed. His name, not theirs as a couple, is inserted on the line. Elsewhere in the offer, usually under "vesting," their intended names as husband and wife should be supplied to the escrow holder and title company.

2. A parent or friend is supplying earnest money for the purchase of a home by others. The parent's or friend's name appears on the first line with the intended buyer(s) names below as vestees. The escrow holder will provide a statement on escrow instructions for the depositor to relinquish any color of title arising out of the depositor's contribution to the funds used to purchase the home.

3. The use of corporate funds to purchase property by an officer of the corporation, usually the owner of a closely-held or solely-held corporation, is not infrequent. When a corporation purchases real property, the escrow holder will want a corporate resolution to purchase, reflected by minutes of a directors' meeting. The name of the corporation must appear on the "received from" line in the offer/receipt.

*   *   *   *

Several comments are appropriate here: Title insurors in most states (check yours) usually "insure around" (exclude coverage of) claims arising out of information not supplied them during escrow by any party—such as who supplied earnest money funds. You have a clear duty as licensee to accurately represent the source of all funds entering the escrow.

Secondly—in many states, funds originating from a joint checking account are deemed to be for the benefit of all parties on the account. We hear frequently of a person in the process of a divorce (yet still married) using joint funds to purchase a home for his or her residence following the divorce. The soon-to-be-former spouse conceivably gains a color of title to the purchased residence. Hello again.

Finally, bear in mind that if the sale falls through, the funds will be returned to exactly the same person who supplied them. Have a clear record in your file. (We suggest a photocopy of the check.)

*   *   *   *

Moving right along: "The sum of $ _____ ." This is the earnest money, expressed in numbers, followed by corresponding words: "$500 (five hundred dollars)," "evidenced by _____ "—cash, check (personal or cashier's), money order or, not infrequently, traveler's check. In most states, acceptance of personal property, foreign currency or promissory note requires disclosure to the seller within the offer form. Be prepared to justify the value and true ownership of personal property. Yankee dollars are just a real nice way to start a transaction.

Caveat: Quite often we all write an offer and execute an earnest money receipt, only to have the offer rejected. We then write a second offer on the same or other property and insert the same earnest money amount. We have, in effect, given receipts for twice the funds actually tendered by the buyers. Very infrequently, we learn of buyers prospering by the confusion that these redundant receipts create, either feloniously or through simple accident.

Suggestion: Request the original offer and receipt back from the buyer for your file or state on second or subsequent offers that the earnest money recited was actually receipted on a prior document.

Nobody said it is easy. . . .

A change in emphasis now, as the language shifts from earnest money to the offering: "For the purchase of real property located at _____ ." This is the address of the listing by street and number, followed by the tax assessor's parcel number or a legal description. The crosscheck aids the escrow holder, particularly in the case of a condominium, where the common street (frequently private) and number is in fact legally known as a unit within a recorded subdivision. Vacant lots pose similar identity problems—the lot between 860 and 880 Bay Street probably won't appear in any records as 870 Bay Street. Finally, *city* is fine, but *county* is mandatory as the basis of origin for legal description.

*   *   *   *

The above information is usually the building block of the offer—we depart here, on most forms, to blank space for terms and conditions of the purchase, but alas, seldom is there enough blank space. To augment that dearth of space, we use the "Addendum" form, requiring little explanation here. Avoid the pitfall of many agents, who try to get the whole offer on the meager space provided in the offer form. Some detail is invariably omitted, to the detriment of one of the parties. Addendums are cheap—follow the lead of one fledgling author of a real estate book, and write to your heart's content, using one or more addendums. (Addenda?!...)

At your side should now rest the *Realty Bluebook©*—the bible of the prudent offer-writer. The *Bluebook* contains clear language for almost any clause you wish to insert and the checklist in the back of the book prompts inclusion of information frequently forgotten in an offer. Veteran salespeople, a decade into the business, continue to use the checklist when completing purchase agreements.

At this juncture, we are (or soon will be) real estate licensees, not bar-admitted attorneys. One of the paramount responsibilities of our profession is to represent our clients with the clearest and most concise contracts possible, while remaining well out of the legal arena (where the boundary lines are frequently hairline and faded).

We advise our clients from the outset of any transaction that we are not attorneys and invite them to have their legal counsel review our work. (In many locales that invitation is imprinted on our standard real estate forms.) We are comfortable using generally accepted verbiage, much of which we take from sources like the *Bluebook* and other handbooks bearing the imprimatur of the various state bar associations. But as the complexity of a transaction mounts, we prefer and occasionally demand that a qualified attorney look over our shoulder at our work.

*   *   *   *

We will regard this chapter as a success if the reader grasps nothing but these two concepts: time limitations (or requirements) on each act of the contract and ceilings on costs, affecting the buyer or the seller. Neither party to the transaction should have any doubt as to the final, worst-case expenditure that is foreseeable at the conclusion of the transaction. Our chore as the licensee is to foresee those costs, absent of rose-colored glasses, represent them clearly and then limit them contractually. Experience teaches that a slight lean toward pessimism is justified in about seven out of ten escrows we open in the current, volatile market we deal in, and while Lord knows we're trying to present a positive approach to this new business you've entered, prudence is paramount when an offer is being written.

*   *   *   *

We'll write an offer for $100,000 on a listing, originate an 80 percent conventional loan, splitting the points with the seller evenly and close July 31, 19 _____ . The seller will supply a pest control report and spend up to $250 to cure conditions revealed in the report. She'll pay for the appraisal. Some minor information in normal offers will be omitted here in the interest of brevity and also because local practice varies and the costs incurred are nominal. (We refer to escrow, title insurance, revenue stamps, recordation and the like—wordy to include and of slim educational value.)

We move now into the blank area of the form, with the above proposed offer in mind:

"A": [Note the use of letters to indicate paragraphs (if your offer form has numbered preprinted paragraphs). Future reference to "paragraph 1" might give rise to confusion as to the "printed" or "inserted" paragraph. "Paragraph A" is clear and unique.]

We'll start again:

"A": "Buyer to deposit into escrow $20,000, which includes above deposit in cash or cashier's check on or before July 30, 19 _____ ."

Analysis: *Which includes* is superior language to the more common *including above deposit*. The latter language infrequently creates the misconception that the earnest money already deposited is over and above the $20,000 down. *Which includes* suppresses the confusion. (And don't forget to move the earnest money to escrow from your broker's trust account prior to the closing date.)

We have contractually bound the buyer to arrange for cash or a cashier's check *prior* to the close of escrow. Marching into the escrow officer's cubicle on closing day with a personal check will probably result in a delay while the funds are verified. Absent the direction on the offer, you will be held out as the culpable party. And cashier's checks ain't what they used to be either—confirm with your escrow officer that an out-of-town cashier's check will be honored without delay. If not, start moving the money earlier.

Confirm that dates selected for an act, i.e., close of escrow, are in fact business days of the week. And when using a number of days less than thirty, be specific as to business or calendar days. The average month has 30 percent fewer business days than calendar days, holidays considered. While we are led to believe that any stated number of days in excess of thirty days is considered to be a calendar day count, we've never seen it in black and white. Take charge and create a rule yourself. Simply spell out the period clearly.

Back there somewhere we stated a down payment, and a concise time and method for deposit. Now the proposed loan:

"B": "Buyer to qualify for and secure a conventional loan in the amount of $80,000 bearing no more than ten percent annual interest for a term of 30 years with a monthly payment not to exceed $702.06 per month, including principal and interest. This offer is contingent upon securing such loan and buyer shall make application for loan within five business days of acceptance of offer."

Analysis: The type of loan has been revealed, with an amount borrowed, maximum interest rate, term and maximum payment stated. We state interest as *no more than* to allow the buyer-borrower to take advantage of a windfall interest reduction should that occur in the escrow interim. Ditto the monthly payment—reduced to track the interest. Early in your career, form the habit of following payments, in offers or anywhere else, with the letters *PI*—principal and interest, or *PITI*—PI plus taxes and insurance. (Occasionally, in a condo or town-house, you'll use *PIT* if hazard insurance is included in the associa-tion fee.)

Inasmuch as the buyer is making an offer contingent upon acquir-ing financing, we bind him to start the process within a stated number of business days—five is usually reasonable. Occasionally, we state within the offer that the buyer has been "prequalified" by a lender. That language is more relevant to marketing than proper offer-writing, which is what we're about in this book, but the prequalification lan-guage is worth observing.

The language above is fairly elementary. The underlying financing theory and discussion—fixed versus variable rates, conventional/FHA/VA programs, buydowns, protective equities (loan-to-value) and so on, are complex and vary from area to area and from the time these words were written to the time you are looking at the book. For these reasons we admittedly skirt a comprehensive discussion of financing and implore you to use some face-to-face sources as you write your initial, or fiftieth, offer.

Now a few terms and conditions to insert in the offer:

"C": "Buyer and seller to share equally in loan discount points, if any, to a limit of (?) total points. If total points exceed (?), this offer shall be voidable by either party and earnest money shall be returned to the buyer."

Analysis: We have limited the exposure of either party to excessive points. We might write the offer in, say, a two-point market, and pre-pare the parties that points could rise to three or fall to one. In a vola-tile market the points might go sky-high on closing day. A ceiling is necessary because an inordinate rise in points will usually deter one party from performing their obligation. Nobody likes that eventuality, but be realistic—we've seen points go to eight. If the buyers don't have four loan discount points' cost, plus the origination fee, plus all the other costs of the sale in the bank, they can't close anyway. Even though she can't close the escrow, the sharp agent can at least alter it using predetermined options.

We chose, quite arbitrarily, an equal point split. The concepts above apply to any division of loan point obligation. Sometimes we've asked the seller to pay one and the buyer the balance to a limit of (?), or we've had one party pay them all (again, to a limit). The point is to be ready for unheralded bumps in the economy and write an offer defensively, for all the parties.

"D": "Seller shall at his expense provide a clear pest inspection report into escrow and shall spend up to $250 to clear deficiencies revealed in that inspection."

We preface the analysis with the thought that we chose *pest control report*, but could well have used structural, mechanical, soil, septic system, well or any other type of report asked of the seller by the buyer. (Similarly, we could have indicated that the buyer would be obligated for payment.)

Clear in the language is the liability to pay for the report and the action to be taken when it is prepared. Note—the requirement is made with total disregard as to how or when the report is done or when the repairs will be done (prior to close of escrow). We, as the selling agent, could care less if the Bug Man sprinkles pixie dust around the crawl space and the report then appears in escrow. The listing agent is deemed to have access to the home and the owner's schedule—it seems appropriate that he orders and arranges for the inspection, no matter who is paying for it at close of escrow.

The seller in the example is limited to spending $250 (an arbitrary amount) to cure defects. If the cost for the cure exceeds that amount, the contract is voidable. In another situation, we might have included, "Seller to pay the initial $250 to cure defects, buyer to pay up to an additional $250 if necessary, to an aggregate limit of $500 total contribution by the parties to effect cure, and if such defects exceed that amount, this contract shall be voidable." (Dollar amounts are examples and variable to suit the case situation.)

A phrase seen frequently that scares us is, "Seller to pay $____ to cure defects and the buyer to pay any additional costs necessitated." Why the trepidation, you ask? Read on:

At Lake Tahoe, California, in the early 1980s, a contract about a structural report read: "Initial $500 to cure deficiencies shall be paid by seller and any additional to be paid by buyer."

The repairs to the home necessitated by the engineer's report amounted to an astronomical $8,000 and some change—a total surprise to all. The sellers, who were well within the letter if not the spirit of the contract, demanded that the buyer compensate them for the repairs (which were completed) and then go into title.

A ceiling on either party's liability would have brought them back to the table for a little renegotiation.

Anticipate the worst and protect both parties. You and your employing broker, as professionals, have a clear exposure to civil remedies sought by buyers or sellers should you let either get themselves into a pickle like this.

* * * *

A clause frequently requested by buyers is the so-called walk-through, wherein they are granted the right to revisit the soon-to-be-theirs home shortly before the close of escrow. When writing an offer containing this clause or when we are the recipient of an offer requesting one, we are quick to point out to all parties the intent of the inspection: to ascertain that the home is in the same or superior condition as it was when the offer was made.

Certain defects appear in any occupied home. The time and place for the buyer to note these problems and demand they be cured is during the showing and offering process. The seller, upon accepting the offer, may acquiesce to making needed repairs.

In practice, many buyers making an eleventh-hour inspection note deficiencies that in fact existed at the time they first viewed the home. Demands are then made by the buyers to cure the defects, as a precursor to closing the escrow.

Buyers, when requesting a walk-through inspection, should be admonished that the only targets of the inspection will be those occurring subsequent to the last time they visited the premises. We advise them that conditions existing now are exempted from cure (notwithstanding warranties contained elsewhere in the offer). We invite them to retour the home for a last, binding look to confirm their perceptions and recollection of the home's condition.

In pages past we held that it is our duty to show the home in its entirety and that we bear a good measure of the burden to point out not only the sweet but the bitter within the listing. Consistent with our broken-record, pedantic caveat to bring problems to the surface when we still have the luxury of time, we strongly advise that if a considerable chunk of the corner brick in the fireplace hearth is missing, that its absence be brought to the buyers' attention. (You'll be pleased to learn that the majority of homebuyers just don't get too excited about smallish shortcomings in an occupied home.)

Our status as professionals makes our duty clear: to entertain a comprehensive definition of the rights of buyers and sellers during a walk-through inspection, to avoid allowing an opportunistic buyer to capitalize on a pre-existing deficiency and hold the escrow hostage. In truth, a seller may adhere to the letter of the contract and decline the repair. In practice, however, most sellers have three-quarters of their possessions in the moving van by the hour the walk-through occurs and are relying on closing proceeds to purchase their next home.

If we explain the walk-through clause properly and word it clearly, our fiduciary-principal will be protected and the buyers will receive equitable treatment from both the licensee and the sellers.

*   *   *   *

One more clause should be covered briefly: When selling their own listings, licensees should include in the body of the offer a disclosure to the effect that "buyer and seller herein are aware that the under-signed agent is representing both parties in the purchase of prem-ises." A dozen variations of the language exist, but recognize the point: Agents in the happy position of selling their own listings are wearing two hats, and during the course of the transaction will usu-ally have to make a decision or offer advice that favors only one of the parties. The disclosure, mandated by a few states, triggers a discussion early in the transaction between all the parties and sets the stage for a few ground rules regarding your obligations.

Within the scope of our simple offer, we've about covered all the bases in the written part of the form, and return now to the preprinted lines to fill in some more blanks. (We expect an avalanche of letters about clauses that we could have written about here. We're not un-aware of the clauses, either, but the scope of the book prevails: some information, augmented by case-basis help to the beginner from local sources.)

Back now to preprinted text: "An approval by the buyer of the title condition within _____ days of receipt of preliminary title report." The opportunity here is for the buyer to read and heed the limitations to the use and enjoyment of their new home, evidenced by deed restric-tions and CC&Rs (covenants, conditions and restrictions). For exam-ple, if the buyer is a radio ham—OK, *amateur radio operator*—the last restriction she wants to see is a prohibition of exterior antennae above the roofline. We usually offer them five business days following delivery of the prelim and then have them initial the report as evidence that they have had the opportunity to review it. A note here—if some change in land use or restriction is due in the area where the buyers have selected a home, we like to state right in the offer something like: "Buyer is aware that proposed extension of LAX runway 31–left will be within 200 feet of subject premises." Execution of the offer demonstrates that the onerous possibility has been revealed to the buyer.

A frequent question in real estate transactions is whether a specific, willful act or, conversely, the absence of the act within an allotted time period demonstrates the parties' acquiescence to a term of the contract. We offer a suggestion: Insert in the language of the offer that "execution of escrow instructions by the parties shall constitute acceptance of the above terms and conditions." In situations where this language will do the job, the clause saves us from keeping track of a myriad of forms and waivers and acceptances, all due at different time stages. The manifold acceptance on escrow instructions frequently, but not all the time, accomplishes the task.

In answer to the question of performance versus lack thereof as acceptance, we don't know, and we get ten answers from ten attorneys. We'll leave that to your case situation.

*   *   *   *

"Escrow opened expeditiously with ＿＿." We like *expeditiously*, but the dinosaur in us recalls that the seller usually pays for title insurance, the bulk of the closing cost. We therefore leave choice of the escrow/title company to the sellers and their agent. "Seller's choice" is a nice request if your form has that blank.

A blank may be available to indicate who will pay for the appraisal, if necessary. Persuasive arguments exist for and against one party or the other paying, as being the benefactor of the report. Splitting the cost down the middle isn't the worst idea in the world.

"Special assessments to be paid/assumed by the buyer/seller." This is a real case-by-case situation, defying discussion without some more facts. We have one warning: We hope that the assessment, if any, is disclosed at the time that the offer is made. If it comes as a surprise in the title search, it may well be paid/assumed by the agent/agents. . . .

"Close of escrow to be on or before ____." Pick a date (on a work day!) mutually agreeable to the buyers and sellers and realistic as to time required for processing a new loan or assuming an existing one. You'll hear bizarre preferences for closing dates—vacations, arrivals of babies, wedding anniversaries, lucky numbers, after the peonies bloom and some even nuttier. We always like to close on the "first." (The "first" chance we get.)

*   *   *   *

Onward. "Title shall be vested in ____ "—a blank with some legal implications. In fact, many forms now imprint the notice to the buyers that their choice of vesting should be made independent of the agent and following consultation with their attorney. Names are of minor consequence—the legal implication arises out of the choice of joint tenancy, common tenancy, severalty and community property in states where that choice is recognized. Some forms follow the vesting blank with the imprint or nominee. Many sellers resist this option, inasmuch as they want to know to whom their property is being sold, particularly if they are participating in owner-financing. If the words cause any party anxiety, we simply line out nominee and have the parties initial the deletion.

*   *   *   *

"Expiration"—the implications of the deadline to accept the offer are split between this offer chapter and later in the acceptance segment. At this stage, we express a date and hour by which acceptance of the offer must be communicated back to you, the agent. Nothing complicated here—if the sellers are in town, we usually give them a day or two to respond. If they reside out of town, another day seems reasonable. But we never allow them ten days to accept just because they're bobbing around Mexico on the Love Boat—you'll be surprised at just how well ship-to-shore radiotelephones work when a listing agent is looking at an asking price offer.

Hindsight is wonderful—we now wish that we'd included in the listing or preparation chapters a suggestion to have sellers planning extended vacations execute a power of attorney to a trusted person somewhere in captivity (never the salesperson) to insure a timely acceptance of viable offers. Maybe we'll include that in the sequel.

*   *   *   *

"Possession shall be granted ____ ''—usually at close of escrow. We personally abhor early possession, but unique circumstances sometime justify rental back to the buyer prior to close. The chosen date of possession is minor as compared to the more significant necessity of regarding the buyer as a tenant, with the possibility in the back of your mind that escrow may not close. A businesslike lease arrangement is demanded, with rental amounts stated and machinery in place to guarantee restoration of possession to the owner. Liability for insurance and utilities must be established and the condition of the premises determined prior to granting custody and control of the home to the tenant/buyer. We usually make reference to the earnest money deposit in the *lease/rental agreement* (the operative document prior to COE). Indicate that the earnest money shall be considered as prepaid rent and/or damage and security deposits for the benefit of the lessor/seller.

*   *   *   *

"Personal property to be conveyed ____ .'' Here, include personal property indicated in the listing, plus anything the buyer wants to have remain with the house. Some counseling and assessment of fair play is usually required here. Wise old brokers kid that an article should always be included that the buyers, in truth, could care less about actually having as their own. This inclusion offers the sellers a chance to scratch the item out with great gusto, satisfying their inner need to show the buyers who's boss, but without materially affecting the larger scope of the transaction.

The obverse situation: We have written offers wherein we have contractually bound the sellers to remove some of their clutter from the premises prior to their departure.

Here now is a small tip: When writing an offer on a home with an oil-fired furnace, include under personal property "fuel oil remaining in tank at close of escrow." Note that we're not making a demand for any specific quantity, or warranting that any will even be in the tank at COE, but burner oil is personal property with a value and should be mentioned in the offer. The inclusion falls under Breckenridge's Rule I: Solve a problem when you still have the luxury of time—if the parties want to negotiate, do so upon acceptance of the offer and not in the escrow officer's cubicle on closing day.

Breckenridge's Rule II: An oil-heated home will always be luxuriously warm and toasty during the last week that the sellers own it.

*   *   *   *

The preceding personal property paragraphs reinforce the need for a phrase we try to include in our offers: "Listing #123456–87 is appended to and made a part of this offer." The amenities, statements and motivational language within the listing that we relied upon to sell the home are thereby affirmed by the sellers if they accept the offer. If personal property was included in the listing, but not specifically addressed in the offer, it is presumed to be integrated into the offer.

*   *   *   *

The next sequence—execution by the buyers. The "selling agent" line is for you, if you are empowered by your broker to sign. Offers should include (but most don't) over the signature line: "Earnest money received by ＿＿＿＿" for in fact that is your primary reason for signing. All too often we see agents sign the line, then drop off the offer at the buyers' home for their signature. Don't sign it until you have earnest money funds in hand.

Integral to your name is your office name as it appears with your state licensing bureau. If the form isn't preprinted with your office name, address and phone number, then include them. We include our home phone number for the other agent's convenience.

Now signatures from the parties making the offer to purchase the home—their usual signature, followed by a printed translation, if necessary. For escrow, middle names are beneficial, even when they don't customarily use a middle name or initial. Follow with a present address and telephone number.

Heighten your attention to detail if the offer is executed by an attorney-in-fact empowered by a power of attorney. Secure a copy of the power of attorney. She executes with her name "as attorney-in-fact for _____ ,'' (the buyers' full names). Determine who will execute forthcoming documents if the offer is accepted.

We suggest that your broker or manager be advised when powers of attorney are used in a purchase offer or any other real estate transaction.

*   *   *   *

And while you're in the manager's office, check up on another occurrence that arises at this point in the chronology. Buyers will occasionally announce, after you have prepared the offer, that they would like to take it to another person for a second opinion.

We mentioned in a earlier chapter that we welcome the opinion of an attorney and if that's where the unsigned offer is destined, so be it. We try to persuade the buyer to allow us to take the offer to the attorney and promise to do so by the crack of eight the next morning. Delivering the offer to the attorney of the buyers' choice perpetuates procuring cause, saves the buyers a trip and keeps the document from floating around town for another day or two.

We do have a problem with the buyers taking the offer to an unlicensed friend, she who has just bought a home, who has just read a book (like this one!) and who will probably undo all the work that you did right in her zeal to display her deep and newfound knowledge of our business.

The final possible critic in the buyers' minds may be another licensee. During our tenure as a community college instructor, seldom a semester went by that a student didn't bring us some real estate document to check out and pass judgment on. As a REALTOR® subscribing to a Code of Ethics, we couldn't look at the thing long enough to see what color paper it was printed on—we'll not offer an opinion that would possibly be held out as a denigration of a compadre's work. We hope that as you grow from novice to veteran you'll share our disdain for this sort of thing.

The question for the sales manager—and there's no clear-cut answer—is what policy your office may have and how best to keep unsigned offers from leaving the building. Happily, the request is made very infrequently and seldom presents an insurmountable problem.

*   *   *   *

As we near the end of the preprinted and inserted clauses of the offer form, the intent of the buyers and their expectations from the sellers should be substantially complete. While the examples and purchasing options here are not totally explored, hopefully a state of mind has been established by the reader as a foundation for real-life situations. To amplify the endless conceivable scenarios would be like playing Trivial Pursuit® without the dice.

We offer finally a method of "proofing" an offer—try this as a standard: A comprehensive and contractual offer-to-purchase document, when executed by the buyers and then executed with no alterations by the sellers, should be contractually complete and enforceable as against both parties without one pen-stroke or spoken word necessary to clarify or embellish it. If explanation is required or information remains to be supplied in escrow, that hole should be plugged prior to execution by the parties.

* * * *

Some counseling is now in order. The buyers hopefully will go now to the aforementioned motel pool and wait out the pins and needles. Not infrequently, buyers with one offer in the mill will make an offer on another home. They are imperiled if both offers are accepted. If they try to write the second offer with you, advise them of that problem—if they persist, which they are entitled to do, collect separate earnest money for each offer.

This happens more frequently than you might realize, typically with clients who want to cover their bases and ensure purchase of a new residence prior to boarding a plane to go home. Writing the backup offer is fine, and frequently is productive, but we suggest you keep the backup in your briefcase until the initial offer flies or dies.

Another topic of counsel is "buyers' remorse." Tell them that they'll surely awaken tomorrow morning wondering if they did the right thing—whether they *really* want the home. Tell them they're not the first buyer, nor the last, to have the anxiety—that we all get the butterflies after we sign. If you've done your job, the home is perfect and will still be tomorrow. Anticipated, preplanned and scheduled remorse is seldom overwhelming.

* * * *

We must now physically convey the contract to the listing agent's office, or another location mutually acceptable to both of you. If we can't find her, we run, not walk, to her office location and give it to someone there with such flair that our delivery will not soon be forgotten. Let no one deny that we did, in fact, deliver a time-limited document.

Some carelessness creeps into the process, frequently to the detriment of the owners and clients whose hopes are now high and to the detriment of the agents, who do this thing for a livelihood.

A recollection of personal experience: We have heard dozens of times that another agent is in the final throes of writing an offer on one of our listings. Implied in this message is that, if a hard offer is received, the rumored offer should be awaited for simultaneous consideration by the seller.

The sad fact is that about nine-tenths of the proposed offers never materialize.

A debate will rage until doomsday about whether an anticipated offer should be revealed to the seller and a decision about a received offer should be postponed until the other, rumored offer is available. (Which it may never be.)

Following some experience with these unkept promises, we formulated a policy: An offer on our listing is an offer when it is received, signed, at our doorstep. This is not to say that we won't chain up and drive five miles to you in a raging blizzard if you're snowbound with an offer. Nor is it to say that if you are ten minutes from delivering it to us, that we won't accommodate you. But don't tantalize us merely over a buyer's strong interest in the home—we like signatures and a deposit.

This is only one office's policy, and quite possibly flawed. Check with your own manager if you are put in this uncomfortable position.

*   *   *   *

It's probably written somewhere that the selling agent has the clear duty to deliver the offer to the listing agent. A fact: We all get paid together, at the same time. We win together or we lose together. If you have an offer on our listing and your car's in the shop, call our office. We'll be there in five minutes to pick it up and keep the transaction moving. We know you'd do the same for us. If the deal closes, you can buy us a burger for our trouble, which beats pride making us both eat crow.

In the normal course of events, we try to get the offer to the listing agent personally. Second best, we get it to his office with the afore-mentioned flair so it isn't buried, only to expire unread. Then we call his home (remember the AD we rely on so often?) and tell him that an offer is awaiting him back at the store. The deadline clock is running. . . .

*   *   *   *

It's been a long day and a long chapter. Trail off home now and let the listing agent do her job. Remain somewhat available to receive a coun-teroffer or the good news of the acceptance.

We've examined in this chapter only one simple type of offer—a new-loan purchase. Variations exist. We'll next follow the offer we write through the counter or acceptance process.

This chapter was written from the perspective of you acting as the selling agent—the offer-writer. A mental shift is required now—you become the other agent—the listing agent. Your phone is now ringing. It's your office—there's an offer on your desk.

Let's go handle it.

13

"We Have a Contract!"

To our knowledge only one man ever made an offer that nobody could refuse. His name was Marlon Brando. He seldom discussed real estate and as we recall the liquidated damages for breach were formidable. Lacking the client control that the Godfather had over his associates, we'll examine what happens to the offer that soared like an eagle from our office, only to land like a turkey in the sellers' nest.

* * * *

A chapter ago we acted as the selling agent, writing the offer. Now we're the recipient—the listing agent, seeing the document for the first time, with the sand ever flowing down the hourglass with two short days to go.

One of four events will occur soon: The offer will expire or will be accepted unchanged or declined or tendered back to the buyers in altered form. As we move through the pages, many of the steps taken and actions required will be common to one, two or more of the four eventualities.

* * * *

We usually look at several key lines of any offer when we receive it prior to getting down to the juicy part—the offering price.

The first glance is for signatures—the buyers', as to legibility, and the other agent's signature and office name.

Regarding the buyers' signatures, we confirm that they have not been made by an attorney-in-fact acting in the true buyers' stead. In that instance we demand a copy of the implied power of attorney from the selling agent to confirm that we're not launching a ship that may sink right after it leaves the ways. We owe that to our sellers.

We confirm that the selling agent's signature appears on the offer for two reasons: first, as prima facie evidence that earnest money has been received and is available to be deposited into the broker's trust account upon acceptance of the offer. The second reason is that in many states a licensee must have demonstrated involvement in the transaction by joining in the execution of the offer, before the state regulatory body will become involved should a code of practice be broken during the sale process.

We look next at the earnest money amount tendered and urge you to talk to your manager about what follows: In many listings, a *"minimum earnest money"* is recited. In the mind of some brokers, this amount is non-negotiable. A selling agent can alter the asking price and terms in crafting an offer, but many brokers feel that if $500 is stated as minimum deposit, an offer isn't an offer unless at least $500 accompanies it. Some agents withhold presentation of the offer until that sum is available.

A better idea—an agent may present the offer expeditiously as state laws require, then withhold response until the full deposit is available. A lesser deposit should not be sufficient to entice the seller to "turn his hole card," as we say in our gaming state.

Your own broker or manager should be given the opportunity to discuss your office's policy on offers with "short" earnest money.

*   *   *   *

We know that you're excited about the offer, but contain your exuberance for just another minute. Add up the numbers, particularly ones preceded by $$$.

Creative financing notwithstanding, the money paid as a down payment, plus financing assumed or obligated, plus purchase-money notes offered to the seller, plus or minus any other value that comes into the escrow in exchange for a deed, should add up to the number entered as the gross selling price.

Basic math precedes emotional analysis of the offer. Add everything up and if it's out of whack, pick up the phone—find out why. It may be just a typo, and easily explained, but it's still an error requiring justification. Be the sole judge of the gravity of the error and don't let a potential headache get swept under the carpet for the sake of expedience.

If no explanation is available or if the other agent honestly believes that the numbers are valid, you have a larger problem. The buyers may be as confused as you are, and when the error surfaces they may have the right to escape from the deal. Urge their agent to reconvene the offering process and help them all get it straight. If the offer is presented with an error the sellers unnecessarily become involved in the daisy chain and their expectations become channeled by erroneous information. Remember the "proof" of an offer in the preceding chapter— if the document can't be signed as written and stand as an ironclad contract without supplementary explanation, it may prove unenforceable later. We got in hot water with the whole world a decade ago by "grading" an abysmally horrible offer with a red "D–" and "See me after class." We sent it back to the selling agent, unpresented, and she then sent it to everybody but the attorney general in Washington. Looking back, a phone call to her might have been wiser. We recommend the phone call.

* * * *

The final area for preanalytical spot-checking: the expiration date of the offer. If the document has been riding around in the selling agent's car for a day, or delayed in the mail, and has expired, don't present it. Have the selling agent supplement the offer with a note, signed by the buyers, to the effect that "Expiration of offer dated ____ is herein extended to ____."

It happened right here in River City (dollars rounded for clarity). A seller, asking $100,000 for her house, accepted an offer of $96,000 after the expiration date of the offer. The buyers, having tested the seller's resolve, declined her acceptance, citing the delinquent acceptance of their offer. They then reoffered $95,500 and she accepted. The listing agent made up the $500 difference.

While no reader of this book would partake in that level of bush-league real estate, others might, so prepare yourself. If the offer in front of you has expired (or is so close to expiration that presentation and negotiation must be done under duress), have the deadline extended to some reasonable time.

None of this is to imply that you simply write off an expired offer—take the steps necessary to resurrect it. Chances are nine out of ten that the time constraint arose out of purely innocent circumstances and the buyers still desire to continue the purchase effort.

*   *   *   *

Our cursory examination confirms that we have before us an offer, not gibberish masquerading as real estate. Communication to the seller would seem to be in order now.

But not quite.

The textbook sequence for presentation of the offer would be a call for an appointment, at which time all of the purchase details would be presented in context—gross price minus costs, equalling a net at close of escrow. The process seldom takes that path—the sellers usually want to know the purchase price immediately over the phone. The peril therein: Details that follow gross price, those to be revealed in the formal presentation, may make an apparent low offer really quite workable. Conversely, an asking price offer may be diminished significantly by excessive costs and demands made upon the sellers.

Just in case we have to divulge details earlier than we'd prefer, we work up the proceeds prior to calling for a presentation appointment. A low offer may look more palatable if we mention early in the conversation that the costs are also low and the net is well worth considering.

The computation of the net, done at leisure prior to making the call, is elementary and takes five minutes. The alternative is making a knee-jerk estimation with the phone in one hand and a calculator in the other, while the seller on the other end of the line builds up resistance to the offer. A workable offer may well wind up declined over the phone, without a chance for a well-prepared presentation.

We use a standard "Seller's proceeds" form that prompts computation of costs in all the categories of expenses and credits, prorated to a known closing date. With proper loan balance information (the usual variant in escrow) an agent can usually compute to within a few dollars the eventual, actual proceeds.

*   *   *   *

Some selling agents like to be present when their client's offer is presented to the seller, either to pitch benefits not clear on the document or to make sure that we do in fact present it. We welcome agents to join us, so long as they're ready to be there at the seller's convenience and they bring their own car and depart after they've made their presentation, so that we may then talk with our principal in private. We agree in advance that their presentation will be restricted to the binding language contained by the four corners of their contract.

Frankly, after we write an offer, we'd just as soon let the listing agent do her job while we go home and have a beer. She has a rapport with the seller that we don't. Quite often a seller regards the two-agent presentation as a double-team effort and defeat is snatched from the jaws of victory.

This minor bone of contention deserves some attention from your sales manager. Many offices have policies requiring their agents to be present when their offers are opened. Other offices have policies against letting the selling agent go forth with the offer to the seller. Some say state laws permit the selling agent to go if she demands the right to be present. No opinion either way is expressed here—just good luck.

*   *   *   *

Tempus Fugit.

The sellers just couldn't say no—they fairly ripped the offer from our hand and begged for a ballpoint. We accommodated them.

Not a mark save for their signatures was made on the form. It was signed as written by all the parties in ownership. As listing agent, we signed our name and office and entered a date and time. We offered a copy to the sellers. (Have we mentioned that most states require, and courtesy dictates, that a copy of all papers pertaining to a real estate transaction be made available to the parties "expeditiously," following signature?)

We hand-deliver it to the selling office, recognized as the agent's usual place of business in the doctrine of delivery. The selling agent may then call the buyers, presumably still waiting around the motel pool, and tell them they have a new home.

*   *   *   *

A slight variation to the above skit: The sellers reside out of town—execution of the acceptance is dependent upon transmittal of the physical document by mail or air express.

We start with a phone call, with well-prepared proceeds and options gathered prior to making the call. We'll assume they like the offer.

Many brokerage offices in normal residential transactions use a Western Union mailgram from the sellers to accept the offer. The sellers, having heard the details of the offer across a time-zone-plagued nation, may call an 800 number and dictate their acceptance. Western Union then transmits the message or a reasonable facsimile to a location near your town, where a hard copy is placed into the mail to arrive on your desk the following morning. The system works very well if the message is originated by phone prior to about 10:00 P.M. local time in the sellers' locale.

Barring strange circumstances, this mailgram is usually sufficient to constitute interim acceptance while the actual offer is transported to the sellers for execution and return to the listing agent. We usually split the cost of Express Mail or Federal Express to and from our town with the cobroker. It's a small price to pay for the luxury in life of knowing that all parties are contractually bound.

As this book grew from a twinkle in the author's eye to a hundred and sixty-some pages destined to a typesetter, so grew the proliferation of the facsimile machine. "Fax" machines, which are usually available in title companies, many copy centers, brokerage offices and by prearrangement with sellers and agents, enable exact copies of real estate documents to be sent from coast to coast in a matter of minutes. Fax has pushed the Mailgram aside as the communication medium of current real estate practice.

*   *   *   *

Two of the four courses possibly taken by offers—signed as written and expired—have been addressed. Two possibilities remain, and next in line for attention is the offer that is flatly refused by the sellers, without even the prayer of a counteroffer.

Discussion of the rejected offer is brief: If the sellers will neither accept the offer nor execute a document indicating what they will accept from the buyer, then the offer dies at the moment that expiration occurs. But never ceremoniously rip up a refused offer or otherwise burn any emotional bridges when an offer is refused. Sellers have been known to sleep on details of an offer, then call and accept it the morning after they tell you where you can put it (and that's not into escrow). The form is difficult to sign after it's been taped back together and cleaned of coffee grounds and grapefruit rinds.

Final note on refusal of offers—many selling agents demand that the sellers demonstrate their refusal of the offer by scribing *refused* followed by a signature and a date. Some sellers are happy to do this while others are skittish about signing anything at all. If they'd rather not sign, don't press it—it's an unforceable issue and little worth a confrontation. We know of no law that demands a written declination.

*   *   *   *

Here now, the meat of the chapter: the counteroffer form. These pages offer not the theory of this thrust-and-parry mind game of our business, but a simple discussion of the act of properly completing the form. As with other forms in the book, we're now using a standard preprinted counteroffer form.

The counteroffer, or simply "counter," our usual parlance, is the preferred method of changing terms and conditions of an offer. The counter includes an area for signatures of both the parties and, in many areas of the country, a time of expiration after which the counter will not be binding upon the sellers. We should also note that in some areas of the country the form is not in use.

We confess that from time to time we have been guilty of making a simple change in an offer, usually in a noncritical area like an obvious typo, a date falling on a weekend or, most frequently, addition or deletion of personal property. We simply longhand in the change or line out existing words and then have both sides initial it. Use particular care and judgment in these minor changes, if unaccompanied by a true meeting of the minds.

On one occasion where the sellers requested so many departures from the original offer that executing a coherent counter would have been virtually impossible, we completed a fresh *"offer and deposit receipt"* right in the sellers' home. They signed the acceptance line— we then took the offer to the buyers, who, by executing the "buyer" line, completed a binding contract, and we opened the escrow.

In this business, one does what one must.

*   *   *   *

Rule number one in the presentation of offers when a counteroffer is anticipated is to have a counteroffer form with you when you go forth to the sellers for the presentation. Many agents don't.

Rule number two is that the counteroffer is used only to change a well-written offer—an offer that would withstand the test of contractuality if it were signed unchanged. The counteroffer is not a form to use to straighten out a poorly written offer. Way back in the listings chapter we called the listing the trunk of the tree from which the transaction grew. The offer is the same tree in a different forest. If the offer won't fly on its own, a counter to a weak offer may well make it worse. Help the selling agent to proof the weak offer, then use the counter to alter that well-written offer's terms and conditions, if necessary.

*   *   *   *

If the sellers want to change the offer after you present it (the subject of a higher sales price usually arises) we extract from our briefcase the counteroffer form and go to work.

The first act is to boldly write on the offer immediately over the acceptance line: *accepted subject to attached counteroffer*. Then the sellers sign the acceptance line of the offer.

The counteroffer makes reference to the original offer and it is vital that the sellers acknowledge their access and acceptance of the terms and conditions of the offer. For, in fact, any term on the offer not addressed in the counteroffer is deemed to be unchanged and must be accepted on the original. Absent a signature on the offer, the continuity of the contract is threatened and may be held out in court to lack binding effect if problems arise later.

Lines that follow on the counter prompt inclusion of key parts of the offer—the date, parties, premise address—that which makes the offer unique from any other.

Note next preprinted language of the form—(sometimes near the top, but on other forms near the signature area): "All other terms and conditions within the attached offer remain unchanged." We have the sellers initial that area, demonstrating their understanding that if a term wasn't changed on the counter, it stands accepted when the counteroffer is signed.

Next in sequence, the changes—neatly, if you will. We like typed offers and their professional look. Counteroffers, however, are frequently handwritten in the sellers' home during the presentation appointment. The original working title of this book was *Press Hard, You're Making Four Copies*. We decided it was a lousy name for a book, but good advice for making handwritten copies on NCR-paper real estate documents.

As we said above—we'll offer no theory now. Write what you will to your heart's delight and within the sellers' desires. If greed and avarice don't creep into the counteroffer, you might just strike a happy medium between the buyers' and sellers' expectations, and sell the home. It happens that way all the time!

We suggest that after you make the amendments to the offer on the counter form that you proof the counter to cover all the terms impacted by the amendments.

For example, if the price is raised in the counter, then quite probably the down payment and/or the new loan or purchase-money second note must be increased. Arguably, the sellers could care less whether the buyers put down more money or borrow more to cover the higher cost, but an increased loan amount could increase seller participation in the loan discount points.

Ambiguity of intent is a building block for future voiding of the contract you are trying to create. Look past the intent of changes and see the ripple effect they produce. Subject the counteroffer to the same scrutiny and proof that you used to make a good clear offer.

*   *   *   *

We usually counsel the sellers about the effect of the changes they have required and then return to the original offer and go through it, line by line, advising them of what was changed and what stands as written. Frequently in the haste and emotion surrounding the offer/counteroffer process, misunderstandings arise. This crosscheck usually eliminates the confusion.

If we're all in agreement, all parties sign on the lines provided—"sellers" for them, "agent" or sometimes "witness" for you. Date it and time it, and fill in an expiration date and hour. We usually offer buyers less time to accept a counteroffer than we give sellers, primarily because the buyers have usually thought of little else than their top-dollar limit since they signed the offer and seldom take any time at all to either sign the counter or let it lapse.

If your locality uses a form that does not have a blank for expiration of the counteroffer, we urge you to be guided by local expertise, but we'd bet that veterans include an expiration date and hour on their forms. The courts have held that counteroffers with unspecified expirations do not run out to perpetuity, and charge the parties with the responsibility of handling them "expeditiously" within a "reasonable" time. Those terms are somewhat nebulous.

A scenario of the open-ended expiration date should bring the problem into clearer focus: We don't want to give a buyer our bottom-line purchase price, then let him take three weeks to research the market and return to us with a decision. We'd like to see him act in a two-day or three-day period—we owe that to our sellers' sanity.

*   *   *   *

Now holding in your hand a counteroffer signed by the sellers, your activity parallels the selling agent's frenetic dash, this time from the sellers' home to the selling agent's office or home, so that she may communicate the existence of the counter to the buyers.

*   *   *   *

We once encountered a man who was pulling a short length of chain behind him as he walked. When we asked him why he was dragging this chain, he answered that it was easier than pushing it.

Responding to a counteroffer with yet another counteroffer is, in our minds, about as frustrating as pushing that chain. These amendments to amendments rob the transaction of continuity and almost preclude a meeting of the minds.

For this reason many offices have a policy against consideration of counteroffers made in response to a counteroffer. In fact, many experienced agents note in the body of their counters that the "sellers will not consider amendments made to this counteroffer," empowering us, as fiduciary agents to the principals, to demand a new offer if the counteroffer is unacceptable to the buyers.

A fresh offer, incorporating the acceptable segments of the original offer and those acceptable in the counter, then reflecting the buyers' second round of demands, should come close to acceptance by both the parties as their mutual demands become defined in the offer and response. (If this new offer also comes back countered, it might be time to start focusing on another listing!)

By the way, if you start anew on a clean offer, don't forget to reference earnest money already deposited.

*   *   *   *

Shortly after the Magna Carta was signed in 1215 A.D., a salesknave received two simultaneous offers on an English bungalow. The duchess who owned it wanted to make a counteroffer (after she thought about it overknight).

Ever since those early days, the same time-honored question has plagued our business—does a counteroffer have to be shared with all parties who have made a bona fide offer, accompanied by earnest money, on the same listing?

In the ensuing 774 years, we've never heard a firm yea or nay. We've heard persuasive arguments for picking the best buyers to work with and offering them, and them alone, the counter. We've also heard rationale interpreting state laws demanding equal treatment for all legitimate offerors.

This question leads into a short treatise on where we were a few years ago in the business and where we're going. You'll hear of older agents making simultaneous written counters, each counter form admonishing possible buyers that the sellers' acceptance is subject to that buyers' executed counteroffer being the first one back to the listing agent's office. Reread the chapter about notice and fiduciary if necessary, but be guided by the fact that if a counter is signed, in the current opinion of the courts, notice is contemporaneous among the parties. While some practitioners feel that the physical delivery requirement supercedes the court opinions, we counsel the novice salesperson to simply avoid allowing two counteroffers to be in circulation at once.

A response now finding preference in our marketplace is the "request for subsequent offer," a vehicle for sellers to notify all parties that they acknowledge receipt of an offer and for them to identify those areas of the offer that are acceptable and those that are not. The form is somewhat kinder and more businesslike than a verbal rejection and enumeration of what might be more agreeable—these spoken instructions frequently get flipped head over heels as they are relayed from seller to listing agent, to selling agent, then to the buyer.

The written request also allows the listing agent to respond to more than one offer simultaneously, without fear of having three people inadvertently buying the home as with our friends in Marin County and Palo Alto. The ball goes back into the buyers' court(s) and future offers can be dealt with in sequence and on merit.

Our discussion here of the "request for subsequent offer" is purposely brief—be assured you'll hear more about it as it becomes prevalent in your area.

A final note on simultaneous responses to more than one offer, by verbal or written counteroffer or by request for another offer: Withholding the information when the appearance of a discriminatory motivation is possible could cost you and your broker your licenses.

*   *   *   *

A moment ago we used three little letters and we here include a thought that's almost too insignificant to mention, but addresses an inconvenience that occurs just frequently enough to merit attention.

The three little letters are N, C and R. As in National Cash Register, or *no carbon required*. In our area an offer form is commonly used whereon the seller-acceptance line falls dead over the buyer-acceptance line on a counteroffer form also in widespread use. Execution by the seller of one form creates a first-glance impression that the buyer has executed the counter, when the forms are overlaid before signature.

Watch your (non)carbons. Notes, phone numbers, tee times and other doodlings track down, layer by layer, until the final document looks like the bottom of a bird cage.

We once had the honor of entering for the public record in Washoe County an offer to purchase estate property that contained not only the requisite information of address, money, time and commission, but the wheel diameter and tire size for our pickup truck.

District court justices, some a mite crusty anyway, are not impressed by some small-time broker's transportation trivia.

*   *   *   *

A chapter ago we wrote the offer for the buyer then dashed across town to assume the role of the listing agent during this chapter. (We do a lot of dashing about in this business when offers and counteroffers are in the mill.)

Our offer fairly flew into escrow unchanged. Or it took some pulling and tugging, rewriting and shaping, before it was accepted. Another scenario was time running out, but we salvaged it by getting it extended and held that one together, too. Finally, we watched one get wadded up into a tight little ball and slam-dunked into the trashmasher, but we didn't dwell on that one—write clean, comprehensive offers and you'll find that most find their way into escrow. (At this juncture of the transaction, we assure the buyers and sellers of the privity of our contract—that neither the identity of the buyers nor the purchase price will be divulged to others.)

The transaction that we've dissected in the last few hours was professional and well thought out. We put a great deal of time into the listing itself, then did our homework during the preshowing days. We showed it well and fairly, then wrote a good offer or helped the cobroker who wrote the offer.

We presented the offer or counteroffer accurately, and the buyers and sellers now have a firm knowledge of exactly what each has purchased and sold and how much money will pass through their hands on the hour that escrow closes.

This has been an admirable transaction and all the parties will look forward to using your services once again or to referring a friend to you.

*   *   *   *

And best of all, we had a little fun doing it.

Index